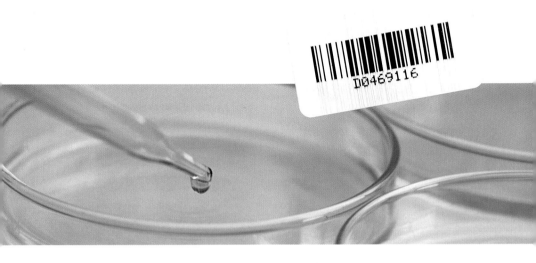

Making the Connections²

A How-To Guide for Organic Chemistry Lab Techniques

Second Edition

Anne B. Padías
The University of Arizona

HAYDEN
HM
MᶜNEIL

ISBN 978-0-7380-4135-3

Hayden-McNeil Publishing
14903 Pilot Drive
Plymouth, MI 48170
www.hmpublishing.com

Padías 4135-3 F11

Table of Contents

What's New to this Edition

The second edition of *Making the Connections* includes a few new sections, in particular ^{13}C-NMR was added, as well as short sections on computational chemistry and green chemistry. End of the chapter problems have also been added to give the students the ability to double-check their knowledge.

The book's aim is still to present the techniques in the organic chemistry laboratory in a straightforward manner, always intending to connect the techniques to procedures we all use in real life, i.e., outside of the lab. The first part of the book deals with the basics of laboratory work, including a discussion about safety, a description of the glassware, and the properties of solvents. The second part explains how to identify the compounds, i.e., how we know what we've made or isolated. Both the physical constant determinations and spectroscopic identification methods are explained. The third part gives details on how to purify compounds, while the fourth combines all of these techniques and explains how to run a typical reaction.

Introduction

Organic chemistry is the science of carbon molecules. Organic chemists identify many compounds from nature, and then synthesize the useful ones or analogs thereof. The "building" of molecules is an essential part of organic chemistry.

The title of the book "Making the Connections" refers to the making of bonds to build these molecules. This book is meant as an instructional tool, and to facilitate the learning process I have included many everyday examples of the chemical principles you will be using in the laboratory. The title is also intended to refer to this aim of "Making the Connections" with the things you already know and understand.

Organic chemistry laboratories have a rather bad reputation as being dangerous. This reputation is still based on a vision of laboratories of about 50 years ago and on the omnipresent explosions whenever the hero in an action movie enters a laboratory. However, as you will find out, working in a laboratory is quite safe. All you need is a little knowledge and *a lot of common sense*.

We have recently become a lot more aware of the short-term and the long-term effects that chemicals might have on the human anatomy. The sweet smell of benzene and the odor of dichloromethane are now forever associated with cancer. Abbreviations such as DDT, PCBs, and dioxins now result in a reaction of fear from most people, and legitimately so. The word "chemical" conjures up a feeling of suspicion, even though everything around us is made up of chemicals in the true sense of the word. Chemistry has brought us society as we know it today, with nylon, antibiotics, painkillers, CDs, computer chips, iPods, brightly colored fabrics, and low-fat margarine. As with everything, a balance has to be found.

In a laboratory environment, many dangers associated with chemistry, and in particular organic chemistry, are amplified. Explosions and fires can happen, but usually do not. For those eventualities, the safety rules are established and will be strictly enforced. Vigilance is always required. Any time people are in a chemistry building, they should be somewhat paranoid and more attentive than in any other building.

An important part of any laboratory course is learning to perform experimental work in an appropriately safe and efficient manner. I am convinced that a basic understanding of the procedures and the logic behind them will help you to perform the experiments in a safe manner. However, as in any high hazard environment, you have to adhere to certain rules. Your own safety will depend on your knowledge of the following rules and regulations. Most of them will already be familiar to you due to your experiences in other laboratory courses, but some will be new because of the unique safety hazards present in organic laboratories.

First the Basics

ALWAYS Safety First

Why?

Safety is important for you, as well as for your coworkers. There are inherent dangers in organic chemistry lab; the chemicals you will work with may be very flammable, and some are toxic. Safety is your number one priority. By working safely and in control of the situation, you not only protect yourself and your classmates, but you also protect the environment from the effect of harmful chemicals.

Which Safety Features Are Available in the Lab?

A laboratory is always equipped with an alarm system and a sprinkler system, which will be activated either when an alarm is pulled or triggered by an occurrence in the building. Each laboratory room is equipped with safety showers, eyewashes, and fire extinguishers. The lab rooms have multiple exit doors to allow for quick evacuation.

If anything goes wrong, your instructor must be alerted immediately. Most emergencies can be handled with available personnel. But if there is any doubt that help is needed, CALL 911. It is much better to err on the side of caution. When calling 911, it is advisable to use a line phone, as most cell phones don't tell the operator where you are located.

The safety shower should only be used if necessary; that is, when your clothing is on fire or if a large amount of chemicals has been spilled on your body and clothing. If this is not the case, it is more efficient to use the faucets and spray heads in the sink. Any contamination of the skin must be rinsed with water for 15 minutes.

If any chemical comes in contact with your eye, use the eyewash station. Hold your eye open with your fingers, and irrigate your eye for 15 minutes. This may seem like a very long time, but taking this precaution is vital to your safety!

The fire extinguisher can be used if there is a fire in the lab. If the fire is in a beaker or flask, it is usually much safer to cover the container and let the fire die due to lack of oxygen. If you are not sure how to use a fire extinguisher, don't do it. If you are not sure that you can extinguish the fire, don't do it. Call your instructor, who has been trained to use a fire extinguisher. Be aware that there are different kinds of fire extinguishers. The most common fire extinguisher in a teaching laboratory is labeled as "ABC," and is appropriate for use in the event of most chemical fires.

Each organic chemistry laboratory is equipped with fume hoods. A hood is an enclosed space with a high continuous air flow, which will keep noxious and toxic fumes out of the general laboratory space. Hoods are often used in teaching laboratories to dispense reagents in a safe fashion. Frequently the workbenches in the laboratory are equipped with either overhead vent hoods or down drafts on the benches itself.

What Should I Wear?

Your eyes are the most vulnerable part of your body. **At all times, you should wear goggles in the lab. No exceptions.** The goggles must be "chemical resistant"; the vent holes at the top of these goggles do not allow any liquid to get inside.

Lots of people wear contact lenses. Accident statistics show that wearing contacts is not more dangerous than wearing glasses in the lab, as long as goggles are worn, but you have to be very aware of the fact that you are wearing these lenses. If an accident occurs and you are wearing contacts, remove them as soon as possible.

Any exposed part of your body is vulnerable to contamination by chemicals. An apron or lab coat should be worn at all times. Shoulders should be covered, so no tank tops without a lab coat.

Closed-toe shoes are also essential. Sandals or flip-flops are not allowed.

The remaining question is: Should gloves be worn or not? There is no denying that gloves play an essential part in lab safety. However, you should be conscious of the fact that gloves are also composed of chemicals, and therefore the right kind of glove should be worn for specific chemicals. Manufacturers of gloves offer information regarding the protection different gloves provide for certain chemicals. Also, it is more difficult to manipulate small items when wearing gloves, and the chances of spills increases with glove use. For most experiments in teaching laboratories, gloves are optional if the chemicals used are not toxic or caustic. Gloves should be worn if indicated in the procedure.

What Should I Pay Attention to?

- No smoking, eating or drinking are allowed in the laboratory. Never taste **anything** in the lab.

- Never leave an experiment in progress unattended, especially if heating is involved. Should you need to leave the lab while an experiment is in progress, get your instructor or a classmate to keep watch over your reaction while you are gone.

- For most experiments, digital thermometers are the best choice. However, for certain experiments, mercury thermometers are irreplaceable. Special rules apply to mercury thermometers because of the highly toxic nature of mercury. If you break a mercury thermometer, do not try to clean it up. You should notify your instructor immediately so that the problem will be taken care of. Make absolutely certain you do not walk through the mercury-contaminated area. You sure don't want to track toxic mercury back to your apartment or dorm room. To avoid breaking a thermometer, secure it at all times with a clamp. Just because you put it in your sand bath, for example, doesn't mean it is secured there!

- If there is a desk area in your lab room, there will be a very clear dividing line between the non-chemical area and the laboratory area. Classroom rules apply to a desk area, while laboratory rules strictly apply once the line into the lab section is crossed.

- Aisles must be kept free of obstructions, such as backpacks, coats, and other large items.

- Never fill a pipet by mouth suction. Avoid contamination of reagents. Use clean and dry scooping and measuring equipment.

- Do not use any glass containers, such as beakers or crystallizing dishes, to collect ice out of an ice machine. It is impossible to see the glass shards of a broken container in the ice, and fellow students could get seriously cut if they put their hand in.

- If the faucets for the deionized water are made of plastic, treat them gently!

- Immediately report defective equipment to the instructor so it can be repaired.

Chemical Waste

One thing to remember about chemicals is that they don't just go away. There-fore, we are all responsible for making sure they get where they belong. There are several waste streams in each laboratory, whether teaching or research: aqueous waste, regular garbage, glass waste, liquid organic waste, solid chemical waste, and special waste streams. We'll discuss all of these in order.

Rule # 1: Only water goes down the drain. It could be soapy water, or it could be very slightly acidic or alkaline, but that's where it stops. NO EXCEP-TIONS! The effluent of the laboratories joins all the other effluent of the city and it is therefore essential that no hazardous materials whatsoever go down the drain.

Regular garbage: All solid non-chemical non-glass waste goes in the gar-bage cans. Lots of paper towels end up here.

Glass waste: All glass waste, in particular Pasteur pipets and other sharp objects, are collected in special containers to avoid harmful accidents.

Liquid organic waste: All organic waste, except the solids, goes into the liquid waste container. This includes the organic solutions generated during your experiments, and all the acetone washings of the glassware. This waste has to be clearly identified at all times with waste tags, and will be disposed of responsibly. These containers have to be capped at all times when not in use, according to EPA (Environmental Protection Agency) rules.

Solid chemical waste: Solid organic chemical waste should be placed into a designated container. This waste includes silica gel from columns, drying agents, contaminated filter paper, etc. It will be disposed of by the laboratory personnel in a responsible fashion.

Special waste streams: For certain experiments, separate specific waste streams will be created. This includes Cr waste from an oxidation reaction or the catalyst used in catalytic hydrogenation. These mixtures require special treatment due to either their toxicity or inherent chemical properties.

The Why and How of a Laboratory Notebook

The Basics About Notebooks

A laboratory notebook is the essential record of what happened in the laboratory. This is valid for teaching laboratories, synthetic research laboratory, or analytical chemistry laboratory. If you do an experiment, you need to write down exactly what you did and what happened. Fellow scientists should be able to read your notebook, and maybe come up with possible alternative explanations for what happened. If a chemist in a pharmaceutical company made the drug taxol for the first time, other scientists might want to repeat this synthesis and potentially improve upon it. To be able to publish experimental results, such as the synthesis of a drug, an official record of these experiments has to exist.

There are some basic rules as far as notebooks are concerned:

- The pages in a notebook are always numbered.

- No pages are ever removed.

- All entries are in ink, and are never deleted. If you change your mind about something, you can always scratch out an entry, but never erase.

- The entries should be dated.

What to Do Before Coming to Lab

First and foremost, you should read and understand the experiment. Read through the description of the experiment, and ascertain that you understand all the underlying chemical principles. If not, look up the chemistry background and study it.

Once you completely understand the experiment, you can start making entries in the notebook. Here is what should appear in the notebook:

- Date

- Title of the experiment

- Objective: What is the purpose of this experiment? It could be to learn a new technique, to examine a reaction mechanism, or to synthesize a compound, or to analyze a mixture, or a number of other possibilities.

- Write the balanced chemical equation, if appropriate. In case of a synthesis reaction, write the starting materials and product. Use the space above and below the arrow to define the reaction conditions, such as temperature and solvent.

A complete balanced chemical equation shows all the reactants, products, catalysts, and solvent and reaction conditions using structural formulas. Also give the molecular weight of each reactant, the amount used, and the number of moles used. For example:

50.0 mL
MW 88, d = 0.806 g/mL
0.46 mol
bp 102°

MW 70
bp 35–38°

MW 70
bp 31°

- The introductory section of your report should contain any physical constant that may be needed to perform or interpret the experiment. For example: molecular weight, melting points for solids, boiling points for liquids, density, solubility, etc. Don't list all constants you can find, only the ones that have a bearing on the experiment. It is convenient and efficient to list the physical constants in table format, as illustrated in Table 1-1. However, quite a few of these physical constants can be incorporated in the chemical equation.

In addition, the safety hazards of the chemicals should be investigated. Information can be found from books or online sources; the MSDS (Materials Safety Data Sheet) will give the most complete information and is obtained from the manufacturer of the chemicals used.

Table 1-1.

Compound	MW	mp (°C)	bp (°C)	d (g/mL)	Safety Considerations
2-methyl-2-butanol	88		102	0.806	
Phosphoric acid					Extremely corrosive, strong acid
2-methyl-2-butene	70		35–38		Flammable
2-methyl-1-butene	70		31		Flammable

- Write the procedure. You should be able to run the experiment using only your outline of the procedure, without the lab manual or a literature article. Your outline should contain enough information to allow you to perform the experiment, but no more. Complete sentences are not needed; a bullet format is preferred. Quantities of materials are required. New procedures may require a rather detailed description, but for familiar procedures only minimum information is needed. In fact, the name of the procedure may suffice; for example, "recrystallize from methanol." Copying the procedure word for word from the original source is unacceptable; summarizing in your own words will be more helpful to you.

Writing the procedure might seem like a waste of time, but doing so will ensure that you know and understand all the steps. Even researchers with decades of experience write out the procedure every time they do an experiment. It might be an abbreviated version with just quantities and keywords, but that is all the information needed to run the experiment.

An easy format is to use the left half of a page to write out the procedure so that you can follow along during lab, and use the right half for recording observations and results on the right side.

What to Write During Lab

When you begin the actual experiment, keep your notebook nearby so you are able to record the operations you perform. While you are working, the notebook serves as a place where a rough transcript of your experimental method is recorded. Data from actual weights, volume measurements, and determinations of physical constants are also noted. The purpose here is not to write a recipe, but rather to record what you did and what you observed. These observations will help you write reports without resorting to memory. They will also help you or other workers repeat the experiment.

When your product has been prepared and purified, or isolated if it is an isolation experiment, you should record such pertinent data as the melting point or boiling point of the substance, its density, its index of refraction, spectral data and the conditions under which spectra were determined.

Figure 1-1 shows a typical laboratory notebook. Note how much detail is given about what really happened during the experiment. The format can vary, and the important thing is to record information during the experiment.

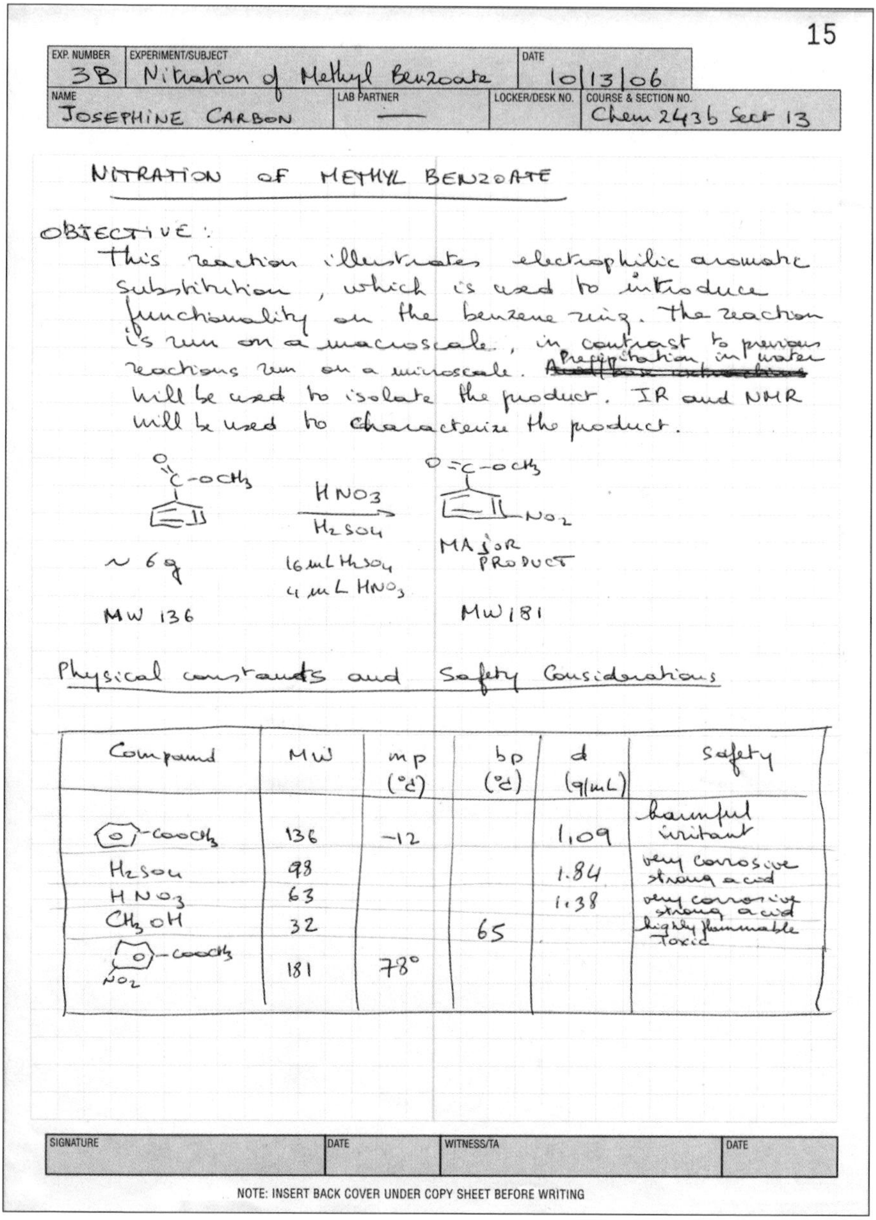

15

EXP. NUMBER	EXPERIMENT/SUBJECT		DATE	
3B	Nitration of Methyl Benzoate		10/13/06	
NAME		LAB PARTNER	LOCKER/DESK NO.	COURSE & SECTION NO.
JOSEPHINE CARBON		——		Chem 243b Sect 13

NITRATION OF METHYL BENZOATE

OBJECTIVE:

This reaction illustrates electrophilic aromatic substitution, which is used to introduce functionality on the benzene ring. The reaction is run on a macroscale, in contrast to previous reactions run on a microscale. ~~A recrystallization in water~~ Precipitation in water will be used to isolate the product. IR and NMR will be used to characterize the product.

~6g   16 mL H_2SO_4 MAJOR PRODUCT

         4 mL HNO_3

MW 136   MW 181

Physical constants and Safety Considerations

Compound	MW	mp (°c)	bp (°c)	d (g/mL)	safety
⬡-COOCH₃	136	~12		1.09	harmful irritant
H_2SO_4	98			1.84	very corrosive strong acid
HNO_3	63			1.38	very corrosive strong acid
CH_3OH	32		65		highly flammable Toxic
⬡-COOCH₃ / NO₂	181	78°			

SIGNATURE	DATE	WITNESS/TA	DATE

NOTE: INSERT BACK COVER UNDER COPY SHEET BEFORE WRITING

Figure 1-1. *Laboratory notebook.*

16

EXP. NUMBER	EXPERIMENT/SUBJECT Nitrobenzoate		DATE	
NAME JC		LAB PARTNER	LOCKER/DESK NO.	COURSE & SECTION NO.

PROCEDURE

- 12 mL H₂SO₄ in beaker and cool in ice bath to ~0°C

- Add ~6 g methyl benzoate d=1.09 → little less than 6 mL in volumetric cylinder

- Cool mixture to 0°C (ice bath)

- Mix 4mL H₂SO₄ and 4 mL HNO₃ and cool to 0°C

- With Pasteur pipet, add acid mixture dropwise SLOWLY Keep temp. <15°C

- Take mixture out of ice bath, warm to room temp.

- ~1 cup ice in beaker

- Add rxn mixture to ice and stir

- filter w/ Buchner funnel

- wash solids w/ 25 ml cold water twice then w/ 10ml cold CH₃OH twice
- weigh
- recrystallize from CH₃OH
- run IR / NMR

OBSERVATIONS

12 mL H₂SO₄ + ~6 g methyl benzoate
ice/water bath

used
5.8 mL methyl benzoate

5.8 mL × 1.09 g/mL = 6.43 g

mixture gets a little warm
Cool in ice bath

Mix H₂SO₄ / HNO₃ → gets warm → cool

Add acid mixture : 1 drop at a time → temp. goes up fast, sometimes up to 20°C
After ~ 1 mL → can add somewhat faster
Addition takes ~ 40 mins.

Pour on ice → ice melts ± white precipitate forms

Filter
wash , put solid in 50 mL beaker
Tare beaker first: 18.56 g
w/solid   23.87 g
          18.56
          5.31 g crude

Recrystallize using ~ 20 mL CH₃OH, filter dry on top of filter

SIGNATURE	DATE	WITNESS/TA	DATE

NOTE: INSERT BACK COVER UNDER COPY SHEET BEFORE WRITING

EXP. NUMBER	EXPERIMENT/SUBJECT Nitrobenzoate		DATE	
NAME JC		LAB PARTNER	LOCKER/DESK NO.	COURSE & SECTION NO.

Tare watch glass 6.52 g
w/ dry solid   10.98 g
       6.52
      4.46 g final yield

m.p. 75.5 - 76.5 °C

IR spectrum using polyethylene card

Place ~ 10 mg in NMR tube. Tube #13
(TA will add $CDCl_3$/TMS).

RESULTS

Theoretical yield calculation
methyl benzoate
  5.3 mL × 1.09 g/mL = 6.43 g

  6.43 g × $\frac{1}{136 \text{ g/mol}}$ = 0.047 mol

m-nitro benzoate   0.047 mol × 181 g/mol = 8.55 g
                      Theoretical yield

Crude yield 5.31 g/8.55 g × 100% = 62.1%

Final yield : 4.46/8.55 g × 100% = 52.2%

m.p. 75.5 - 76.5 (lit. 78°) → not completely pure

SIGNATURE	DATE	WITNESS/TA	DATE

NOTE: INSERT BACK COVER UNDER COPY SHEET BEFORE WRITING

EXP. NUMBER	EXPERIMENT/SUBJECT nitrobenzoate		DATE	
NAME JC		LAB PARTNER	LOCKER/DESK NO.	COURSE & SECTION NO.

Spectral analysis

IR   ~ 3030 cm^{-1} → Phenyl group. C—H
~~3950~~
1723   → C=O ester
1602   → C=C phenyl
fingerprint matches reference spectrum.

NMR.

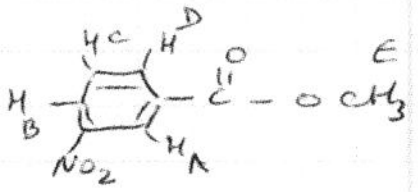

in CDCl$_3$ with TMS

Signal (ppm)	multiplicity	integration	Proton
8.9	s	1 H	H$_A$
8.4	m (maybe q)	2 H	H$_B$ and H$_D$
7.7	m (t?)	1 H	H$_C$ (dd)
7.2	small s	→ CDCl$_3$	
4.0	s	3 H	CH$_3$—O
3.9	small s	?	other isomers ?
2.2	m	acetone trace ?	

conclusion : desired cpd obtained but
not pure —

SIGNATURE	DATE	WITNESS/TA	DATE

NOTE: INSERT BACK COVER UNDER COPY SHEET BEFORE WRITING

What to Write After Lab

First you have to evaluate your data and analyze your results. Some basic calculations will often be necessary, such as % yield and recovery.

In your report you should include the results of the analyses you performed, such as running a TLC plate or measuring a melting point. You should also include any spectra you recorded, as well as your analysis of the spectra. What information can you ascertain from reading the spectra?

You must also draw some conclusions and write a discussion. This is where you demonstrate your understanding of what happened in the experiment. You discuss the results you obtained and draw whatever conclusions you can. Give the proposed mechanism for the reaction in question, if appropriate. Your report can also contain discussion of the following topics:

- What did you expect to happen?

- What actually happened?

- Why did it happen?

- What can explain the differences between your expectations and the actual results?

- What did you learn about the reliability and limitations of the techniques used?

- What did you learn about the reliability and limitations of the equipment used?

- What did you learn about the chemistry?

- How could your results have been improved?

- What could this chemistry or technique be applied to?

The whole purpose of this part of the report is to convince your instructor that you really understand what you did in the lab, and why, and where it can lead to, etc. BE THOUGHTFUL AND THOROUGH!

Finally, make sure you *cite* your data and observations while *explaining* and *interpreting* your result.

Various formats for reporting the results of the laboratory experiments may be used. You may write the report directly in your notebook, or your instructor may require a more formal report that you write separately from your notebook. When you do original research, these reports should include a detailed description of all the experimental steps undertaken. Frequently, the style used in scientific periodicals, such as *Journal of the American Chemical Society*, is applied to writing laboratory reports.

Important Calculations

Laboratory results usually require you to perform some calculations. Here are some examples of calculations that are typically used.

Conversion of Volume to Mass and Number of Moles for a Pure Liquid

Amounts of pure liquid reagents are specified in volume measure (mL or L). To convert volume to mass or to number of moles, use the following formulae:

mass (g) = volume (mL) × density (g/mL)

# of moles = [volume (mL) × density (g/mL)] / MW (g/mol)

> **Example:** We start a reaction with 20 mL of 1-butanol. How many grams and moles does this represent?

> **Solution:** 1-butanol: d = 0.810 g/mL, MW 74 g/mol
> mass (g) = 20 mL × 0.810 g/mL = 16.2 g
> # of moles = (20 mL × 0.810 g/mL) / 74 g/mol = 0.219 mol

Conversion of Concentration to Mass for a Solute

The calculation for the amount of solute in a solvent depends on the type of solution used. The concentration of the solute may be given in several different sets of units, such as weight/weight (w/w), weight/vol (w/v), and volume/volume (v/v). We shall only be dealing with w/v relationships, which can be expressed in terms of molar concentrations or as mass of solute per unit volume of solvent.

a. *Concentrations expressed in terms of molarity:* If the molar concentration of the solute is known, then the following equation is applicable:

$$\text{Solute mass} = M \times V \times MW$$

M = solute molarity in mol/L
V = volume of solution in L
MW = molecular weight of solute in g/mol

> **Example:** Calculate the amount of sodium hydroxide present in 100 mL of a 3.5 M solution of NaOH in water.

> **Solution:** Mass NaOH = 3.5 mol/L × 0.100 L × 40 g/mol = 14 g

b. *Dilution:* To calculate the volume of a concentrated solution needed to make a specified volume of a less concentrated solution, use this equation:

$$M_1V_1 = M_2V_2$$

Where M_1 and V_1 are the initial concentration and volume, and M_2 and V_2 are the final concentration and volume.

Example: Starting from 12 M HCl, how would you make 100 mL of 1 M HCl?

Solution: Use the equation

$$M_1V_1 = M_2V_2$$
$$12 \text{ mol/L} \times V_1 = 1 \text{ mol/L} \times 100 \text{ mL}$$
$$V_1 = 100 \text{ mL}/12 = 8.3 \text{ mL}$$

We use 8.3 mL of the concentrated acid solution and add it to the water to make 100 mL 1 M HCl.

c. *Weight/Volume solutions:* In these solutions, the concentration is expressed in terms of mass of solute per volume of solution. The following equation is used:

$$\text{Solute weight} = C \times V$$

C = concentration of solute in g/L
V = volume in L

Example: Calculate the number of moles present in 250 mL of a solution with a concentration of 240 g of methanol (CH_3OH, MeOH) in 1000 mL of solution.

Solution: Mass of MeOH = (240 g of MeOH/1000 mL) × 250 mL = 60 g of MeOH

# of moles of MeOH = 60 g/(32 g/mol) = 1.875 mol

Percent Yield

Several distinct types of yield calculations are used in organic chemistry lab, always expressed in percentages. The simplest of these yield calculations is the % recovery; for example, in a recrystallization. In reactions, the quantity of material that can be obtained based only on stoichiometry is called the theoretical yield. Organic reactions, however, rarely proceed to completion as shown in the balanced equation.

Competing reactions can consume some of the starting materials, thus reducing the amount of product obtained. In addition, many organic reactions involve equilibrium processes or can proceed rather slowly, and significant amounts of starting materials might still be present at the "end" of the reaction. The amount of material obtained is called yield. A measure of the efficiency of a particular reaction is the % yield.

a. *Determination of % recovery:* In a purification procedure, such as a recrystallization, distillation, or sublimation, the amount of pure material recovered will necessarily be smaller than the amount of impure material you started with. The % recovery is calculated by the following formula:

% recovery = (g of pure material/g of impure material) × 100 %

Example: Calculate the % recovery for the following: 2.5 g of anthracene were recovered after recrystallization of 4 g of an impure anthracene sample.

Solution: % recovery = (2.5 g/4 g) × 100 % = 62.5 %

b. *Determination of the theoretical yield:* Several steps are necessary to calculate the theoretical yield of a reaction. As an example, we consider the acid-catalyzed esterification of 5 g of glutaric acid with 100 mL of ethanol.

1. First we have to balance the equation:

   2 moles of ethanol are needed to convert each mol of diacid to the diester.

   $$HOOC-CH_2CH_2CH_2-COOH + 2\ CH_3CH_2OH \xrightarrow{H^+}$$
   diacid

   $$CH_3CH_2-OOC-CH_2CH_2CH_2-COOCH_2CH_3$$
   diester

   Calculate the number of moles of each starting material and determine the limiting reagent. This information can be added to the equation as follows:

   $$HOOC-CH_2CH_2CH_2-COOH + 2\ CH_3CH_2OH \xrightarrow{H^+}$$

5 g	100 mL
MW 132	MW 46
0.0379 mol	d 0.785 g/mL
	1.706 mol

   $$CH_3CH_2-OOC-CH_2CH_2CH_2-COOCH_2CH_3$$
   MW 188
   Yield 5.80 g

glutaric acid: # moles = $5 \text{ g} \times \dfrac{1}{132 \text{ g/mol}}$ = 0.0379 mol

ethanol: # moles = $100 \text{ mL} \times 0.785 \text{ g/mL} \times \dfrac{1}{46 \text{ g/mol}}$ = 1.706 mol

2. Next, we determine the limiting reagent by examining the stoichiometry of the reaction. Two moles of ethanol are required for each mol of glutaric acid, therefore (0.0379 mol × 2) = 0.0758 moles of ethanol would be needed. The ethanol is present in large excess, and thus the glutaric acid is the limiting reagent.

3. Third, we calculate the theoretical yield based on the limiting reagent and the molar ratio between the limiting reagent and the product. In this case, one mol of glutaric acid leads to one mol of diethyl glutarate, a 1/1 ratio:

   Theoretical yield = # mol of limiting reagent × (mol product/mol starting material) × MW product

   Theoretical yield = 0.0379 mol × (1/1) × 188 g/mol = 7.12 g

c. *Determination of the actual yield:* The actual yield is determined by the direct weighing of the product, in this case, 5.80 g.

d. *Determination of percentage yield:* The percentage yield is given by the following equation:

   % Yield = (actual yield/theoretical yield) × 100 %

   % Yield = (5.80 g/7.12 g) × 100 % = 81.5 %

Basic Lab Techniques

Glassware

In addition to the beakers and Erlenmeyer flasks that you used in your previous labs, organic chemists use a basic set of specialized glassware. This glassware exists in different sizes. The amount of chemicals you use determines the size of the glassware you will use.

Most organic chemistry lab students use a basic assembly of microscale glassware. Why is it called microscale? The reactions are run on a much smaller scale in a teaching environment than in a research or industrial laboratory, where scientists are trying to make large quantities of material for commercial use. The quantities of starting material used in a teaching lab are usually on the 100–500 mg scale. The advantages of smaller-scale experiments are multifold: it is less dangerous when students are working with smaller amounts, running the lab is less expensive, less waste is generated, and it is more ecologically responsible. In research and industrial laboratories the size of the experiment can vary from <1 mg to several kilos.

Glassware used in organic labs has glass joints that fit together very tightly and are used for efficient coupling of different pieces of glassware. You can even pull a high vacuum on an apparatus with glass joints once it is properly assembled. It is essential that both the male and female joints be of exactly the same size to achieve a tight fit and not break glassware. The size of a joint is defined by both the width and the length of the joint in mm, and is called Standard Taper ⏀ (Figure 1-2). The first number refers to the diameter of the largest part of the ground joint, in millimeters, while the second number refers to the length of the ground joint. For microscale glassware, the ⏀ is 7/10. Small-scale glassware (50–100 mL) is usually ⏀ 14/20, while intermediate size glassware is ⏀ 19/22 (250–500 mL). Really big glassware has really large joints, such as ⏀ 45/50.

©Hayden-McNeil, LLC

Figure 1-2. *Example of ground glass joints.*

The basic piece of glassware in an organic lab is the round-bottom flask. Its convenient shape allows for effective stirring and it can be placed under vacuum if necessary. A variation of the round-bottom flask is the conical vial found in many microscale assemblies. Microscale glassware, used in many teaching laboratories, has an O-ring and a screw cap to simplify assembly of the small pieces of glassware.

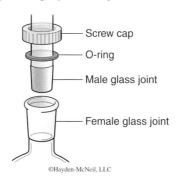

Screw cap

O-ring

Male glass joint

Female glass joint

©Hayden-McNeil, LLC

Figure 1-3. *Microscale connector.*

Other pieces of glassware will be introduced as new techniques are discussed. Treat all this glassware with great care. To prevent glass joints from getting stuck during the experiment ("frozen"), the joints are to be lubricated using a very small amount of stopcock grease. Make sure you disassemble the ground glass joints before storing.

Clean Glassware

Glassware can usually be cleaned easily if it is cleaned immediately. It is good practice to do your "dishwashing" right away. With time, the organic tarry materials left in a container dry out and really get stuck, or worse, they begin to attack the surface of the glass. The longer you wait to clean glassware, the more difficult it will be to clean it effectively. Here are various options:

- A variety of soaps and detergents are commercially available for washing glassware. They can be tried first when washing dirty glassware.

- Organic solvents are often used, since the residue remaining in dirty glassware is likely to be soluble in an organic solvent. Acetone is the most common solvent used for this purpose. Acetone is a very good, inexpensive solvent with high volatility, so it is easy to remove any last traces of acetone by blowing air through the glassware. Warning: acetone is very flammable.

- More aggressive methods such as a base or acid bath can be used if necessary. These methods are common in research labs, but are not often used in a teaching laboratory. Most of these are very caustic and therefore dangerous. A "base bath" is a mixture of KOH, some water, and lots of isopropyl alcohol, while an "acid bath" is usually chromic acid, a mixture of sodium dichromate and sulfuric acid. Less dangerous equivalents of the latter are commercially available. Use extreme caution with any of these options.

Thermometers

Temperature can be measured using different kinds of thermometers.

- Digital thermometers are a rather novel addition to the organic lab, but are much safer than many of the other options. The temperature range of a digital thermometer is from -20 °C to 200 °C, but some thermometers can have a range up to 400 °C. The temperature range of the thermometer has to match the reaction conditions, and the temperature probe has to be resistant to the reaction conditions. For example, some probes might not be able to withstand concentrated acid conditions.

- Mercury thermometers were the mainstay of all laboratories for a very long time. They have a wide temperature range, up to 300 °C. Due to the fragility of these thermometers, coupled with the toxicity of mercury that is released upon breakage, many labs have minimized the use of these thermometers. In case of breakage, make sure you notify the appropriate personnel to clean up the mercury spill.

- Alcohol thermometers can also be used, though they have a limited temperature range of up to 110 °C. They are also fragile, but the contents are non-toxic.

Practical Tips

- The temperature readings are only as accurate as the thermometer you use. It is good practice to occasionally calibrate a thermometer. The easiest calibration method is to double-check the 0 °C reading by dipping the thermometer in an ice bath.

- The thermometer can also be checked by measuring the melting point of known pure compounds. Examples are benzoic acid (mp 122.5 °C) and salicylic acid (mp 159 °C).

- Mercury thermometers measure the temperature by measuring the expansion of the heated mercury in the thermometer; however, only the bottom part of the thermometer is subjected to this temperature, which can cause accuracy problems. Modern mercury thermometers are "corrected," which means that the thermometer has been calibrated with part of the thermometer immersed in the liquid to be measured. If you look closely at the thermometer, you see an etched line ~7 cm from the bottom of the thermometer: this is the emergent stem line; the thermometer should be immersed in the liquid to this level to get an accurate temperature reading.

- Some thermometers are calibrated for full immersion use, such as in heating baths. In this case there will not be an etched emergent stem line.

- Thermometers can also have ground glass joints (taper joints), as shown in Figure 1-4, for use with ground glass equipment for easy assembly.

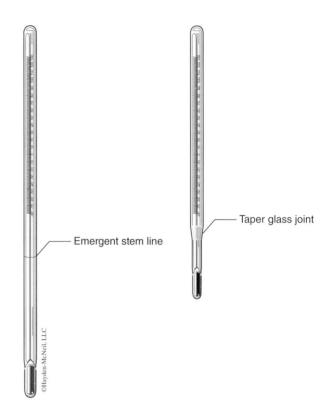

Taper glass joint

Emergent stem line

©Hayden-McNeil, LLC

Figure 1-4. *Different styles of thermometers.*

Weighing Samples

For most experiments, starting materials and/or products have to be weighed. These can be either liquids or solids.

To weigh solids, the following steps are recommended:

- If you need an accurate measurement, a balance that reads at least to the nearest decigram (0.01 g) is needed. In organic labs, balances accurate to the milligram (0.001 g), or even tenth of a milligram (0.0001 g), are common.

- Place the round-bottom flask or Erlenmeyer flask that you are going to use for the experiment in a small beaker, and take these with you to the balance.

- Don't weigh directly into the reaction flask. Instead, place on the balance pan a piece of weighing paper that has been folded once. The fold in the paper will assist you in pouring the solid into the flask without spilling. Tare the paper; that is, determine the paper's weight or push the "zero" feature on the balance.

- Use a spatula or scoopula to transfer the solid to the paper from the bottle, and weigh your solid on the paper. Don't pour, dump, or shake a reagent from a bottle.

- Weigh the solid and record the weight.

- Transfer the solid from the paper to your flask before heading back to your bench. Having the flask in a beaker serves two purposes: it keeps the flask from toppling over, and the beaker acts as a trap for any spilled material.

- It is often not necessary to weigh the exact amount specified in the experimental procedure. It is, however, very important to know exactly how much material you have. For example, if you obtain 1.520 g of a solid rather than the 1.500 g specified in the procedure, the actual amount weighed is recorded and the theoretical yield will be calculated using that amount.

To weigh **liquids**, the procedure is slightly different.

- Weigh the empty reaction flask.

- Calculate the volume of liquid needed based on the density.

- Use a syringe or pipet to measure the liquid and transfer it to the reaction flask. It is essential to use a clean pipet or syringe to draw the liquid from the bottle. Don't contaminate the bottle! Another option is to pour an approximate amount of liquid into a beaker and transfer the reagent from the beaker to the reaction flask using the syringe or pipet.

- Weigh the reaction flask again to determine the amount of reagent in the flask. Again, the most important thing is to know how much material you start with rather than matching the exact amount given in the procedure. The amount should be in the same range as the given procedure.

Measuring Volumes

The method used to measure a volume largely depends on the accuracy needed. In the organic chemistry laboratory, some volumes are very important while others are not as crucial. An analogy is cooking spaghetti: when you cook the spaghetti, you don't have to worry about measuring the exact amount of water used: the amount of water should be large enough so that the spaghetti doesn't stick, but you don't want to use too much water because then it will take forever to boil. When it comes to the spaghetti sauce, however, it is important to have a more exact measurement of the salt you add, or the results could be disastrous. The same is true in the organic chemistry laboratory: some amounts have to be exact, while others, like the amount of solvent used in refluxing (boiling) a reaction mixture, do not, as long as you are in the correct concentration range.

Beakers or Erlenmeyer flasks should never be used to measure an accurate volume, as the volume markers on this glassware are not at all exact. Volumetric cylinders are more accurate and are often used to measure rather large amounts. The volume has to be read correctly; the exact volume corresponds to the bottom of the meniscus. For more accurate measurements, use graduated pipets or syringes. For small volumes, syringes are very accurate and convenient. Figure 1-5 shows methods for measuring volumes.

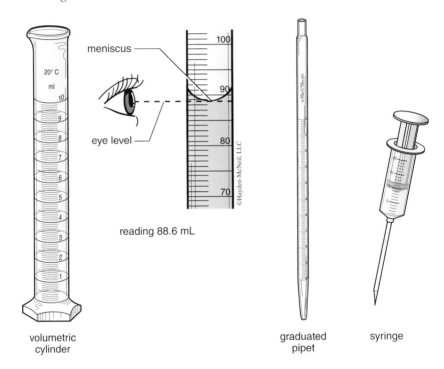

Figure 1-5. *Methods for measuring volumes.*

Heating Methods

Many organic reaction mixtures need to be heated in order to complete the reaction. In general chemistry, you might have used a Bunsen burner (open flame) for heating because you were dealing with non-flammable aqueous solutions. In an organic chemistry lab, however, you must heat non-aqueous solutions in highly flammable solvents. In general, you should never heat organic mixtures with a Bunsen burner.

Many alternatives to Bunsen burners exist, such as:

- **Heating mantles:** These units are designed to heat round-bottom flasks of varying sizes. The inside is usually fabricated from a mesh material, and the heating controls are built into the unit.

- **Thermowells:** They have a ceramic cavity designed for a specific size flask; a 250-mL thermowell is very common. The thermowell has to be connected to a rheovac, which controls the power and therefore the temperature of the flask. To adapt to smaller glassware, sand can be placed into the well. Just remember to use a minimum amount of sand, as sand is a bad conductor of heat (Figure 1-6).

- **Hot plates with or without magnetic stirring:** Hot plates can be used to heat flat-bottomed containers. NEVER heat a round-bottom flask directly on a hot plate: you are heating only one little part of the flask that way, creating a lot of stress on the glass leading to failure; the flask can break and not only do you have shattered glass, you have a shattered experiment, as well! Erlenmeyer flasks, beakers, and crystallizing dishes can be heated on hot plates.

- **Water baths with hot plate/stirrer:** This heating method can be used if the required temperature is below 100 °C. Water baths are very convenient because they are non-toxic and non-flammable, and the temperature is rather easily maintained.

- **Sand baths with hot plate/stirrer:** This heating method can be used for higher temperatures. Keep in mind that sand is a poor heat conductor; therefore, a minimal quantity of sand should be used.

- **Oil bath with hot plate/stirrer or heating coil:** Different kinds of oil can be used, each with different heat stability. The more expensive silicone oils are more heat resistant. With cheaper Ucon oils, you have to keep in mind that they are flammable.

- **Aluminum block with hot plate/stirrer:** An aluminum block is specialized equipment often used in teaching labs that use microscale glassware (Figure 1-6).

- **Steam baths:** These have fallen into disuse, as hot plates and other methods are much more convenient. Older labs were often equipped with steam lines.

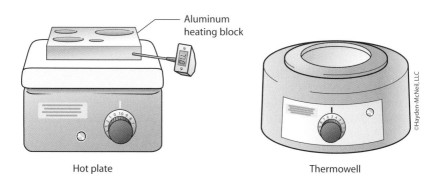

Figure 1-6. *Heating methods.*

Cooling Methods

Some reactions are highly exothermic and therefore should be run at a low temperature. Low temperatures may also be necessary to control reaction products. Cooling solutions can also increase the yield of crystals in a recrystallization. Cooling of a solution might have to occur slowly or quickly, depending on the circumstances.

A cold bath can be any of various containers, such as beakers or crystallizing dishes. Dewar flasks are double-walled insulated containers, which maintain a low temperature for a much longer period than a simple beaker.

Depending on the temperature needed, different cooling methods are used:

- Ice/water baths are the simplest and are used to maintain temperatures between 0 and 5 °C. Finely-shaved ice is most effective, but has to be mixed with water, as ice alone is an inefficient heat transfer medium.

- Ice/salt mixtures (3 parts ice/1 part NaCl) can reach a temperature of –20 °C.

- Acetone/dry ice or isopropyl alcohol/dry ice mixtures maintain a temperature of –78 °C.

- Liquid nitrogen is at –195.8 °C or 77.3 K.

- Dewar flasks should be used for the last two cooling methods, because these low temperatures are difficult to maintain.

- Use caution when handling either dry ice and liquid nitrogen: insulated gloves should be worn to grab a block of dry ice, and safety glasses or goggles are a necessity when filling Dewar flasks with either dry ice or liquid nitrogen.

Generating a Vacuum

In many instances, such as vacuum distillation or sublimation, lower pressures are necessary to run an experiment. How do we generate a vacuum? It depends how low the pressure has to be. To obtain low-pressure, vacuum conditions, one of the following methods can be used:

- A water aspirator is cheap and effective, but limited by the vapor pressure of water at room temperature. Therefore, the maximum vacuum that can be obtained with a water aspirator is ~15 mmHg, depending on the temperature of the water.

  Water aspirators connected to the city water supply have one major disadvantage: as the water is washed down the sink, trace amounts of the solvent being evaporated are swept down the drain and into the sewage system. The use of water aspirators can lead to pollution, and in some jurisdictions, water aspirators are not allowed.

  Self-contained water aspirators are commercially available. These systems have their own water supply and minimize water waste. The advantage is that contaminated water is contained and can be disposed of properly as chemical waste. The other advantage is that the water bath can be cooled with ice, which results in a better vacuum and lower pressure (Figure 1-7).

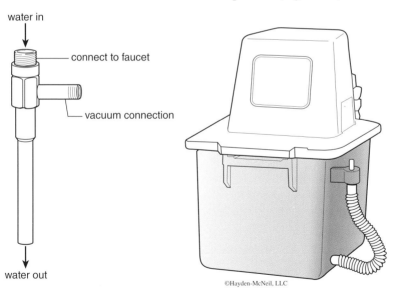

Figure 1-7. *A vacuum aspirator and a self-contained system.*

6

- For lower pressures, vacuum pumps can be used. These vary from little mechanical pumps to high vacuum oil pumps. Pressures of as low as 0.01 mmHg can be obtained with these vacuum pumps. Some laboratories might have house vacuum.

- When using vacuum, you must always install a cold trap. The trap is cooled with either a dry ice mixture or liquid nitrogen, to trap unwanted vapors before they reach the pump. The content of the trap should be disposed of as chemical waste.

Filtration

There are two basic forms of filtration: gravity filtration and vacuum filtration. Either one of these can be performed at room temperature or at high temperature (hot filtration).

Let's deal with room temperature filtration first. If the material to be filtered is rather granular, gravity filtration works just fine. For example, removing a drying agent from 50 mL of a solution is easily accomplished using gravity filtration. The setup for gravity filtration is shown in Figure 1-8. An Erlenmeyer flask or filtration flask is equipped with a funnel. The funnel is supported by an O-ring. A filter paper is placed in the funnel; it can be either fitted or fluted (see Figure 1-8). The fluted filter paper results in a larger surface and faster filtration. Overall, gravity filtration is rather slow.

Vacuum filtration is an effective method for filtering powders in large or small amounts, and it is faster than gravity filtration. A Büchner funnel with a filter paper is used in conjunction with a filter flask, as shown in Figure 1-9. Büchner funnels are made either of porcelain or plastic. A filter flask has a side arm and, because it has to withstand vacuum, it is made of durable, thick glass. A neoprene adapter or a rubber stopper with a hole is used to form the seal between the funnel and the filter flask. The setup is connected to the house vacuum or any other source of vacuum, like a water aspirator or vacuum pump, with a thick-walled vacuum hose.

For microscale filtration (<20–300 mg), a Hirsch funnel is more appropriate, because it minimizes product losses (Figure 1-9). It is made of porcelain and fitted with a small filter paper. A neoprene adapter is used to form the seal with the filter flask. The filter flask is connected to the vacuum source.

For really small amounts (<50 mg), use a Craig tube, which is described in the section on Recrystallization (Chapter 3).

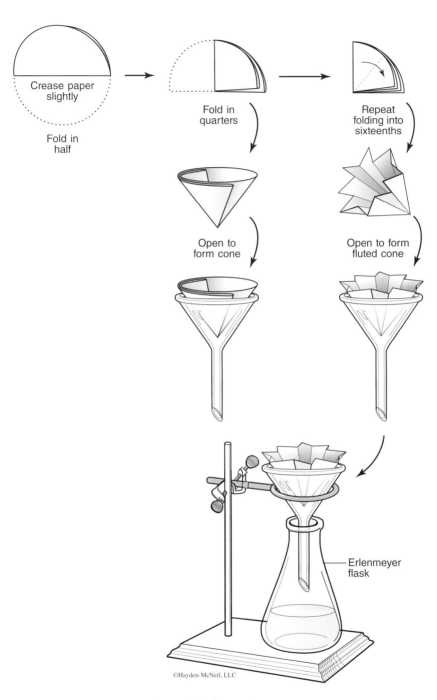

Crease paper slightly

Fold in half

Fold in quarters

Repeat folding into sixteenths

Open to form cone

Open to form fluted cone

Erlenmeyer flask

©Hayden-McNeil, LLC

Figure 1-8. *Gravity filtration.*

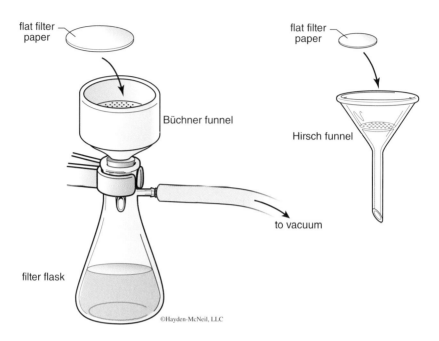

flat filter paper

Büchner funnel

filter flask

flat filter paper

Hirsch funnel

to vacuum

©Hayden-McNeil, LLC

Figure 1-9. *Vacuum filtration.*

To remove drying agent or other solids from microscale solutions (<10 mL solution), Pasteur pipets fitted with cotton plugs are very efficient and help minimize loss of material (Figure 1-10). The Pasteur pipet is suspended and a small cotton ball is inserted right at the narrowing of the pipet. Don't use too much cotton, or glass wool, as it will act as a plug and slow down filtration significantly. You want just enough cotton to hold back the solids.

For even smaller volumes to be filtered (<1 mL), a filter pipet can be used in which a little bit of cotton is forced in the narrow part of the Pasteur pipet using a thin copper wire (Figure 1-10). This filter pipet can be used relying on gravity, or the solution can be forced through the cotton plug by applying pressure using a pipet bulb. This filter pipet can also be used to pipet liquid out of a solid/liquid mixture, leaving the solid behind; it is almost like a reverse filtration.

And now let's discuss hot filtration. Hot filtration is most commonly used when purifying a compound by recrystallization (see Chapter 3). The compound X to be purified is soluble in a solvent at high temperature, while the impurity Y is not. The most efficient way of removing the impurity Y is to filter the solution hot, while compound X is in solution. Any of the techniques described above for room temperature filtration, vacuum and gravity, can be used for hot filtration. The complicating factor is that compound X will most probably crystallize out as the solution cools during filtration. Because vacuum filtration is fast, it can be used to avoid this problem. Another option is to keep the filter, and therefore the solution, warm; specialized equipment has been developed over the years to achieve this, but it can be as simple as insulating the filter with cotton wool.

Practical Tips

• Use the appropriate size filter paper to exactly fit the Büchner or Hirsch funnel.

• For vacuum filtration, first turn on the vacuum, then wet the filter paper with a minimum amount of solvent before pouring the solution on the filter: this helps the paper to form a nice seal with the Büchner or Hirsch funnel.

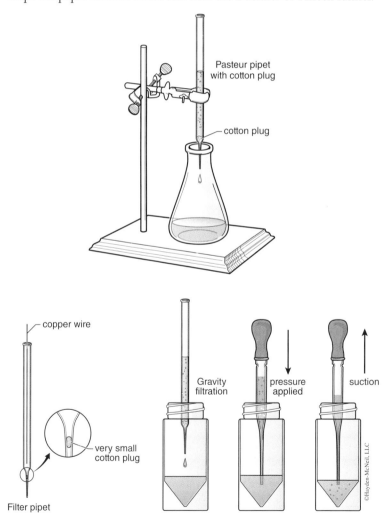

Figure 1-10. *Micro-filtration.*

- Use vacuum tubing for vacuum! Vacuum tubing has very thick rubber walls so the tubing won't collapse on itself when submitted to vacuum. If you use tygon tubing, normally used for cooling water, the tubing will immediately collapse, and you won't achieve any suction.

- Use a cold trap between a vacuum pump and the filter flask. If using a water aspirator, an empty trap prevents water from backing up into your filtration flask.

- Make sure you securely clamp the filtration flask. They tend to be very top-heavy and tip over very easily.

- Leave the vacuum on for a while after you finish the filtration; this way, you pre-dry the crystals thanks to the continuing air flow.

- Always disconnect the filtration flask before turning off the vacuum.

Basic Reaction Setup

There are a variety of basic reaction setups to choose from, and the setups you use depend on the purpose of the procedure and also on the scale. For large quantities, >50 g or mL, "standard" scale glassware is used, and these glassware pieces usually have ground glass joints for easy assembly (see Figure 1-2). For miniscale (<50 g) or microscale (<1–2 g) procedures, smaller versions of this glassware are used, but the basic principles are the same. The microscale glassware in particular is very compact, and the ground glass joints are equipped with O-rings and screw caps for easy assembly (Figure 1-11). The microscale setups will be discussed if they are significantly different from the macro- or miniscale setups.

Screw cap
O-ring
Male glass joint
Female glass joint

©Hayden-McNeil, LLC

Figure 1-11. *Microscale round-bottom flask.*

The setup for a reaction should be adapted to the specific circumstances. The size of the glassware used is determined by the size of the reaction. Will the reaction be cooled or heated? Will the reaction need protection from air? Is it moisture-sensitive? Is it oxygen-sensitive? Is the solvent volatile? Will reagents be added during the reaction? The answers to these questions will help you decide on the particular apparatus to use. We discuss a few simple setups here, which can be modified depending on the circumstances.

Reflux

Many reaction mixtures have to be heated for the reactions to proceed at a reasonable rate. The solvent is usually chosen so that its boiling point coincides with the ideal reaction temperature. If you heat the mixture to reflux, you are assured of a constant appropriate temperature. For example, if you want a reaction temperature of ~60 $°C$, tetrahydrofuran is a very appropriate solvent (bp 65 $°C$), but if you want slightly above 100 $°C$, toluene would be a great choice (bp 110 $°C$).

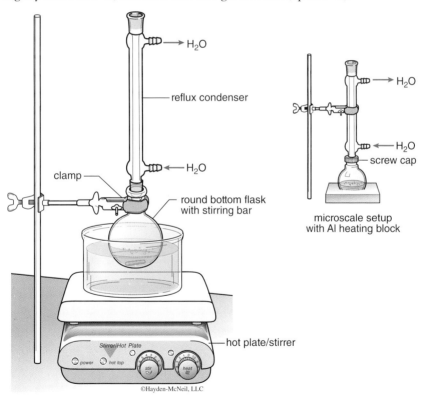

reflux setup with water bath

Figure 1-12. *Refluxing.*

To achieve reflux (boiling), a round-bottom flask is equipped with a reflux condenser and the mixture is heated. The detailed setup again depends on the size. The round-bottom flask should be at least twice the size of the total volume of the reaction. The reflux condenser is water-cooled, or can be air-cooled if you are using a very high boiling solvent and reagents.

To prevent bumping, boiling chips or boiling stones should always be added to the solution. Always add the boiling chips before heating the solution. Boiling chips are usually carborundum (compound of carbon and silicon), which is chemically inert. The boiling chips are porous; liquid migrates inside the pores and gets heated, forming bubbles. The chips also provide sharp edges for the bubbles to form; a glass round-bottom flask is just too smooth for effective bubble formation, which can lead to overheating of the solution. A stir bar can also serve as a nucleation point for bubble formation.

Controlled Atmosphere

Many reactions are very sensitive to moisture or oxygen or both. Anhydrous conditions can be maintained using a drying tube. A glass tube filled with a drying agent will prevent any moisture from contaminating the reaction. This drying tube is most often placed on top of a reflux condenser.

The drying tube can take many forms: it can have a glass joint, or it can be connected using a thermometer adapter. It can be as simple as a Pasteur pipet filled with drying agent, with cotton plugs at both ends. Some examples are shown in Figure 1-13.

In case of anhydrous reactions, the glassware is oven-dried prior to assembly or flame-dried using a large Bunsen burner.

If a reaction is even more sensitive and cannot be exposed to air, the reaction has to be run under nitrogen or argon. After flushing the setup with the inert gas, it is advisable to maintain a positive pressure. Continuously passing the inert gas through the reaction results in excessive evaporation of any volatile material, solvent or reagent. As shown in Figure 1-13, in this case a Claisen head can be used, one end of which is equipped with a reflux condenser. The other end is linked to a gas cylinder via a glass T joint. The third end of the T is connected to a bubbler. Before the reaction is started, the reaction flask is flushed with the inert gas: it goes in through the Claisen head and exhausts through the reflux condenser. Once the reaction has started, the reflux condenser is capped off with a septum, and positive pressure is maintained on the system by the oil present in the bubbler. A slow bubble rate ensures that no outside air can enter the reaction setup.

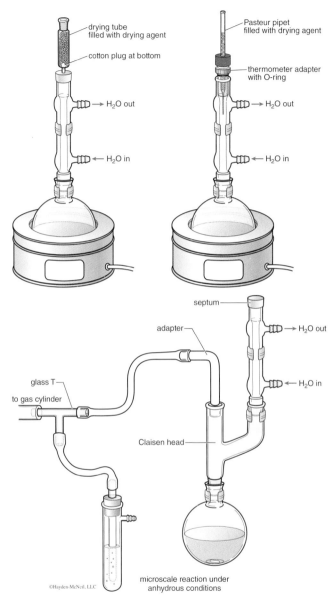

drying tube
filled with drying agent

cotton plug at bottom

→ H₂O out

← H₂O in

Pasteur pipet
filled with drying agent

thermometer adapter
with O-ring

→ H₂O out

← H₂O in

septum

adapter

glass T

to gas cylinder

→ H₂O out

← H₂O in

Claisen head

©Hayden-McNeil, LLC

microscale reaction under
anhydrous conditions

Figure 1-13. *Reactions run in anhydrous conditions.*

Addition of Reagents During the Reaction

Sometimes all reagents can be mixed at the beginning of a reaction, but at other times one or more of the ingredients have to be added at a slow and controlled rate. Liquids can be added using either an addition funnel or a syringe. Again, the detailed setup depends on the size of the reaction. Flasks with multiple necks (joints) or Claisen heads can be used to accomplish these additions.

For rather large-scale reactions, a three-neck flask is very commonly used. One arm is equipped with a reflux condenser, while another can be used for an addition funnel. The reagent, or a solution of the reagent, can be added at a very slow rate using the stopcock of the addition funnel. The addition funnel often has a pressure-equalizing tube so that it can be stoppered. The third neck of the flask is commonly stoppered, but could be used for other purposes if necessary. A common setup is shown in Figure 1-14.

For microscale setups, the situation is a bit more complicated (Figure 1-14). Because the round-bottom flasks are so small, it is not practical to have more than one neck. Claisen adapters provide the added arms necessary for addition and reflux. In this case a syringe is used instead of an addition funnel because the syringe accommodates the smaller quantities and provides control of the addition rate. The Claisen head can be either below or above the reflux condenser, depending on the circumstances.

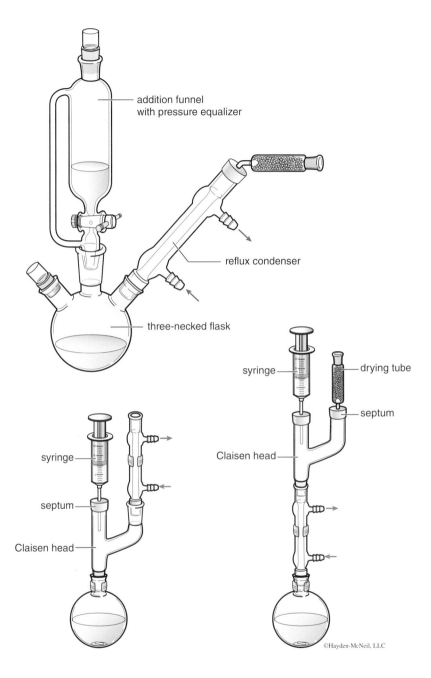

addition funnel
with pressure equalizer

reflux condenser

three-necked flask

syringe

drying tube

septum

Claisen head

syringe

septum

Claisen head

©Hayden-McNeil, LLC

Figure 1-14. *Addition of reagents.*

Dealing with Noxious Fumes

Often reactions result in noxious fumes. To keep the atmosphere in the laboratory at a tolerable level, these reactions have to be vented in an efficient manner.

For large-scale reactions and in research laboratories, all reactions should be done in the hood. However, some chemicals should not be vented into the atmosphere. For example, if HCl is formed during a reaction, this acid should be neutralized and not sent up the hood. To accomplish this, the outgoing gas stream is sent through a neutralizing solution, which can be in a trap or an Erlenmeyer flask (Figure 1-15).

In a teaching laboratory environment, the number of hoods is often limited and it is not possible for all students to run their reactions in those hoods; the hoods' use is limited to dispensing of reagents and collection of waste. In this case, a small funnel mounted above the reflux condenser and connected to an in-house vacuum can alleviate many of the pollution problems in the laboratory.

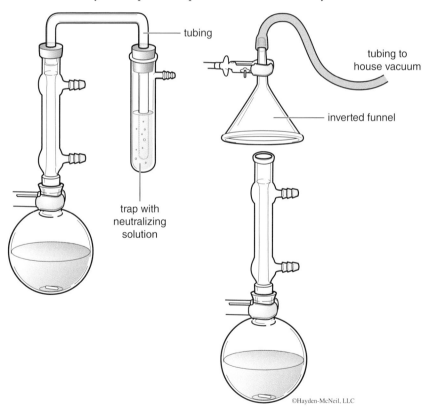

©Hayden-McNeil, LLC

Figure 1-15. *Controlling noxious fumes.*

Solvents

Solvents play several crucial roles in the organic chemistry laboratory. They are used to dilute the reagents in reactions, to control the reaction temperature (reflux), to recrystallize compounds, and in chromatographic applications, just to name a few. It is essential to have a sound understanding of the role of the solvent, as well as of the interactions of the solvent with the reagents and solutes. The following section aims to clarify these issues.

Melting and Dissolving

What is the difference between melting and dissolving? Even though these two terms are often used interchangeably in common English, in a chemistry laboratory the two are fundamentally different. A candy that melts in your mouth doesn't really melt; it actually dissolves in your saliva (water)—unless it is chocolate, of course!

Melting is a phase transition a solid undergoes when heated. On a molecular level, the regular crystal structure of the solid is lost when the solid melts, but the intermolecular distance between the molecules doesn't really change a lot.

Dissolution of a solid, however, is very different. When a solid is dissolved in an appropriate solvent, the solvent molecules surround each individual molecule or ion. The same is the case when a liquid is dissolved in a solvent. The ability of a particular solvent to dissolve a particular solute depends on the intermolecular forces between the solvent and solute molecules.

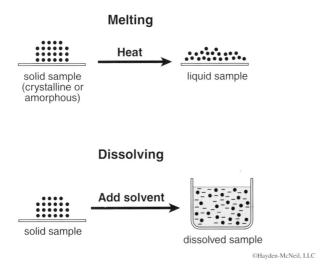

©Hayden-McNeil, LLC

Figure 1-16. *Difference between melting and dissolving.*

Polarity and Intermolecular Forces

The polarity has a significant influence on the ability of a specific solvent to dissolve a specific solute (the dissolved compound). The fact that a compound dissolves in a solvent shows that there are interactive forces between the two kinds of molecules. For example, water is a good solvent for both table salt (NaCl) and for table sugar (sucrose), but on a molecular level this is due to completely different intermolecular forces: NaCl will dissolve because of ion-dipole attractive forces between the Na cations and the Cl anions with the dipoles of water, while sucrose dissolves mostly because of the hydrogen bonding between the sugar and the water molecules. Intermolecular forces are the forces of attraction that exist between molecules in a compound, and therefore they affect the solubility of one substance in another. Intermolecular forces are generally much weaker than covalent bonds. Here are the different kinds of intermolecular forces in order of decreasing strengths (Figure 1-17):

- **Electrostatic forces** occur between charged species, cations and anions, and are responsible for the extremely high melting and boiling points of ionic compounds and metals.

- **Hydrogen bonding**: a hydrogen atom in a polar bond (e.g. H–F, H–O or H–N) can experience an attractive force with a neighboring electronegative molecule or ion that has an unshared pair of electrons (usually an O or N atom on another molecule).

  Hydrogen bonds are considered to be dipole-dipole interactions (see below) and are quite polar. The hydrogen atom has no inner core of electrons, so the side of the atom facing away from the bond represents a virtually naked nucleus. This positive charge is attracted to the lone pairs of an electronegative atom in a nearby molecule. Hydrogen bonds vary from ~4–25 kJ/mol, so they are weaker than typical covalent bonds. But they are stronger than dipole-dipole and/or dispersion forces. Hydrogen bonds are extremely important in the organization of biological molecules, especially in influencing the structure of proteins.

  A very good example of hydrogen bonding is H_2O. It is unusual in its ability to form an extensive hydrogen bonding network. Each water molecule can participate in four hydrogen bonds, one with each non-bonding pair of electrons and one with each H atom. The boiling point of water illustrates the dramatic effect of hydrogen bonding on boiling points. Water has a molecular weight of 18 g/mol and a boiling point of 100 °C. The alkane nearest in size is methane; with a molecular weight of 16 g/mol, methane boils at −167.7 °C! There is no hydrogen bonding in methane.

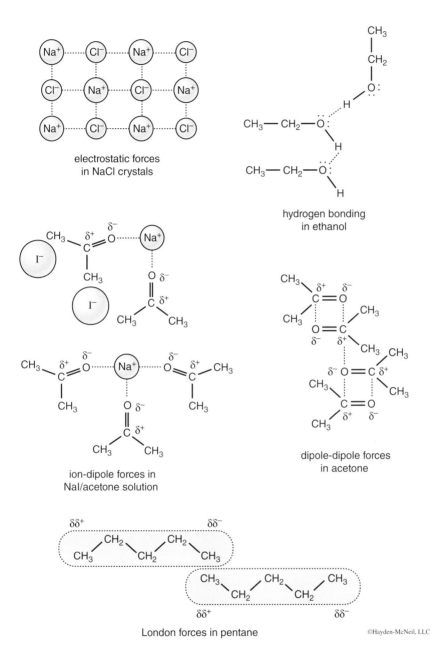

electrostatic forces
in NaCl crystals

hydrogen bonding
in ethanol

ion-dipole forces in
NaI/acetone solution

dipole-dipole forces
in acetone

London forces in pentane

©Hayden-McNeil, LLC

Figure 1-17. *Intermolecular forces.*

The hydrogen bonding ability of water allows it to effectively dissolve chemical compounds with hydrogen bonding ability, such as the sucrose mentioned above.

- **Ion-dipole forces** involve an interaction between a charged ion and a polar molecule (a molecule with a dipole). Cations are attracted to the negative end of a dipole, while anions are attracted to the positive end of a dipole. The magnitude of the interaction energy depends upon the charge of the ion, the dipole moment of the molecule, and the distance from the center of the ion to the midpoint of the dipole. Ion-dipole forces are important in solutions of ionic substances in polar solvents, such as table salt in aqueous solution.

- **Dipole-dipole forces:** Polar covalent molecules, such as aldehydes and ketones, have the ability to form dipole-dipole attractions between molecules. Polar covalent bonds act as little magnets; they have positive ends and negative ends which attract each other. Polar molecules attract one another when the partial positive charge on one molecule is near the partial negative charge on the other molecule. The polar molecules must be in close proximity for the dipole-dipole forces to be significant. Dipole-dipole forces are characteristically weaker than ion-dipole forces and increase with increasing polarity of the molecule.

- **London forces:** All molecules have the capability of generating London forces. Non-polar molecules would not seem to have any basis for attractive interactions, but Fritz London (1930) suggested that the motion of electrons within an atom or non-polar molecule can result in a transient dipole moment. London forces are solely dependent on the surface area and the polarizability of the surface of the molecule. These are the only types of forces that non-polar covalent molecules experience. They result from the movement of the electrons in the molecule, which generates temporary positive and negative regions in the molecule.

Solubility and Solvent Strength

The common adage "like dissolves like" is valid in many instances, but many other situations can also occur. "Like dissolves like" implies that a solvent is effective as a solvent if it has a similar structure to the solute. For example, 1,3-dichlorobenzene is very soluble in chloroform.

Based on our knowledge of the possible intermolecular forces, we can easily conclude that the solvent can also be very different from the solute and still be an effective solvent. Acetone, for example, dissolves such disparate compounds as sodium iodide, acetic acid, benzene, and hexane.

Many reactions are run in solution to bring the reactants together and to control the reaction conditions. Solvents are also used in purification and isolation techniques. For all these applications, it is essential to clearly understand the properties of the solvent used.

A word of warning: Avoid contact with organic solvents as much as possible. Upon repeated or excessive exposure, some may be toxic or carcinogenic (cancer-causing), or both. It is also essential to remember that most organic solvents, with the exception of the chlorinated solvents, are flammable and ignite if they are exposed to an open flame or a match.

The polarity is a crucial factor when a solvent has to be chosen for any application, be it as the solvent for a reaction, or for extraction, chromatography, or recrystallization. Table 1-2 lists the properties of many common solvents. The dielectric constant ε is a good measure for the polarity of the solvent. Other factors to be considered are the boiling point, melting point, and the density of the solvent. Also, is it flammable? Is it toxic? Is it inexpensive?

Different compounds will have unique solubility behavior in various solvents (Figure 1-18). As a rule, solubility will increase with temperature, but exceptions to this rule are known: for example, the solubility of NaCl in water does not really increase with increasing temperature.

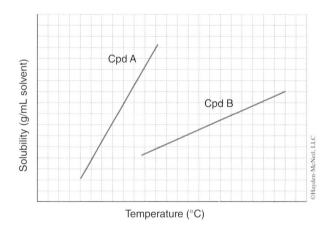

Figure 1-18. *Solubility curve.*

Table 1-2. Properties of Common Solvents

Solvent	Dielectric Constant (ε)	bp (°C)	mp (°C)	Density (g/mL)	Comments
Water H_2O	80	100	0	1.0	• For very polar compounds • Not miscible with most organic solvents
Methanol CH_3OH	33	65	−98	0.81	• Good recrystallization solvent for highly polar compounds • Crystals dry fast • Highly polar solvent for chromatography
Ethanol CH_3CH_2OH	24	78	−117	0.81	• Very versatile solvent • Higher boiling than methanol • Less polar than methanol
Acetone $(CH_3)_2C=O$	21	56	−95	0.79	• Very polar solvent • Dissolves almost any organic compound • Highly polar solvent for chromatography • Very flammable
Dichloromethane CH_2Cl_2	9	40	−97	1.34	• Very good solvent for chromatography, extractions, and recrystallization • More polar than chloroform • Not flammable
Tetrahydrofuran $(CH_2)_4O$	7.6	66	−108	0.89	• Extremely versatile solvent • Medium polarity • Reasonably chemically inert • Available in anhydrous form

Solvent					Notes
Ethyl acetate $CH_3-CO-OCH_2CH_3$	6	77	-84	0.90	• Semi-polar solvent for chromatography and recrystallization • Nice smell • Flammable
Chloroform $CHCl_3$	5	61	-63	1.49	• Versatile solvent for chromatography and recrystallization • Medium polarity • Not flammable
Diethyl ether $(CH_3CH_2)_2O$	4	35	-116	0.71	• Very versatile solvent for reactions, extractions, recrystallization, and chromatography • Very low boiling and very flammable • Available in anhydrous form commercially • Medium polarity
Toluene $C_6H_5-CH_3$	2	110	-95	0.87	• Non-polar solvent, very effective for chromatography and recrystallization • Flammable
Hexanes C_6H_{14}	~2	68–70		0.67	• Isomer mixture of hexanes is cheaper than pure n-hexane • Very non-polar solvent used for chromatography and recrystallization • Flammable
Petroleum ether	~2	35–60		0.64	• Hydrocarbon mixture composed of mostly pentanes • Very non-polar solvent for recrystallization • Flammable

Problems for Chapter 1

1. Draw a map of your laboratory classroom and indicate where the safety features are located.

2. Why should shoes be worn in a laboratory?

3. Assess the hazards of the following chemicals using either books or on-line sources to find this information:

   a. Methanol
   b. Sodium sulfate
   c. Toluene
   d. *n*-Butyl lithium
   e. Tetrahydrofuran

4. Discuss three issues related to the use of gloves in a laboratory.

5. Look up the molecular weight, boiling point, melting point, and density of the following compounds:

   a. Cyclohexane
   b. *t*-Butyl bromide
   c. Potassium iodide
   d. Limonene

6. Assuming a reaction is run between 0 and 100 °C, determine which physical constants collected for Question 5 will be relevant to the chemist running this reaction.

7. Calculate the following:

   a. Weight of 100 mL cyclohexane
   b. Weight of 0.01 mole potassium iodide
   c. Volume in mL of 0.01 mole limonene
   d. Number of moles in 30 mL *t*-butyl bromide

8. Describe how to make 100 mL 0.01 M aqueous KI solution.

9. What is the % recovery in the following scenario: student A purifies 1.63 g of crude bromocyclohexane by distillation and obtains 0.60 g of pure product.

10. For each of the following reactions, calculate the theoretical yield and % yield. Don't forget to determine the limiting reagent.

a.

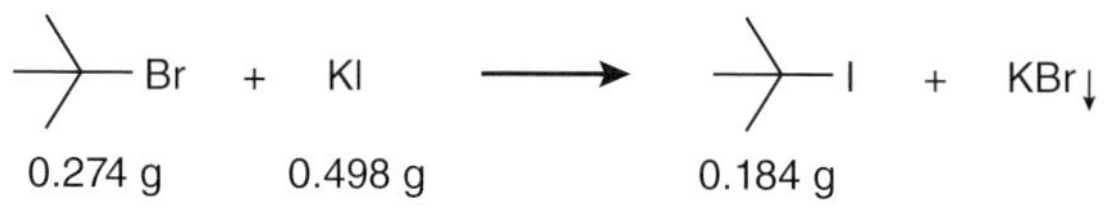

    0.274 g   0.498 g   0.184 g

b. 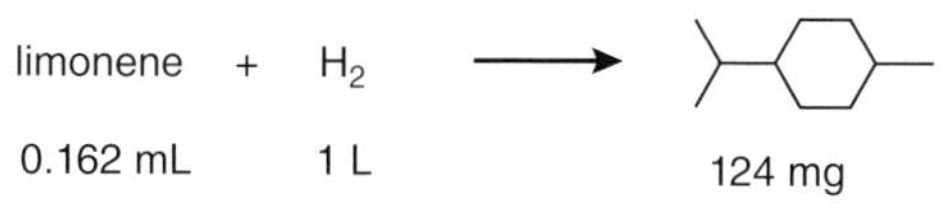   limonene + H_2

    0.162 mL   1 L   124 mg

c.

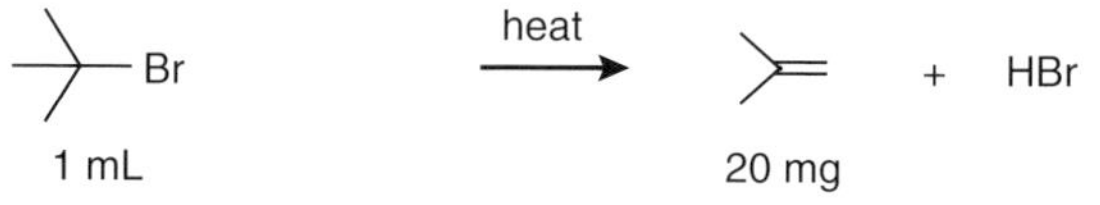

    1 mL   20 mg

11. Which heat source might you use to heat the following solvents to reflux? Look up the boiling points first.

   a.   Methanol
   b.   Toluene
   c.   Hexanes
   d.   Diethyl ether

12. Among the following solvent pairs, which layer would be on top? Or would they be miscible?

   a.   Hexane and water
   b.   Water and ethanol
   c.   Ethanol and chloroform
   d.   Water and dichloromethane
   e.   Acetone and toluene

13. Consider the polarity of the following solutes (dissolved compounds) and solvents, and predict which compounds would have a good solubility in the proposed solvent:

   a.   Acetic acid and water
   b.   Sodium sulfate and acetone
   c.   3-Pentanone and ethyl acetate
   d.   Potassium bromide and toluene
   e.   3-Ethylhexane and dichloromethane
   f.   3-Ethylhexane and water

14. Arrange the following molecules in order of increasing polarity

15. Identify the major intermolecular force in pure samples of the following molecules. Arrange in order of increasing polarity.

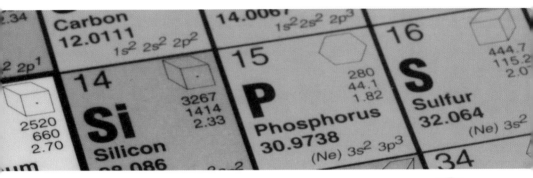

.34 Carbon
     12.0111
        $1s^2\ 2s^2\ 2p^2$

2 $2p^1$

     14

          3267
          1414
2520 Si 2.33
660
2.70 Silicon
um   nº 086

14.006
        $1s^2\ 2s^2\ 2p^3$

15

     P   280
            44.1
            1.82

     Phosphorus
     30.9738
        (Ne) $3s^2\ 3p^3$

16

S   444.7
       115.2
       2.0

Sulfur
32.064
   (Ne) $3s^2$

34

How to Identify Compounds

The physical properties of a compound are those properties that are intrinsic to a given compound when it is pure. Often, a compound may be identified simply by determining a number of its physical properties. The most commonly recognized physical properties of a compound include its color, melting point, boiling point, density, refractive index, molecular weight, and optical rotation.

The knowledge of the physical constants of all chemicals used in a reaction is essential to be able to make informed decisions in the laboratory. Is a compound a liquid or a solid? Is it volatile? Is it polar? Is it toxic? How will I dispose of it? When faced with a procedure, you have to decide which physical constants are important, and which are of no consequence. For example, if using acetone as a solvent, the following information can be found in the literature: MW 58, b.p. 56 °C, m.p. −116 °C, d = 0.791 g/mL, n = 1.359, it is an irritant and it is flammable. For reactions done at room temperature, the boiling point is important because we could lose the solvent if the reaction mixture is heated too high. However, the melting point of acetone is of no consequence in this case, because it is out of the range of normal reaction conditions. The density of acetone is important, but its molecular weight is not significant. On the other hand, if acetone is used as a reagent, its molecular weight must be known. It is always important to know if a compound is flammable and if it could have any health effects.

Many reference books list the physical properties of substances. Physical properties of substances can be found online, most notably on *Chemfinder.com* and on the Sigma-Aldrich Website (*sigmaaldrich.com*). Useful books for finding lists of values for non-spectroscopic physical properties include:

- *Aldrich Catalog*

- *The Merck Index*

- *The CRC Handbook of Chemistry and Physics*

- *The Dictionary of Organic Compounds*

- *Lange's Handbook of Chemistry*

- *CRC Handbook of Tables for Organic Compound Identification*

Modern chemists also include the various types of spectra (infrared, nuclear magnetic resonance, mass, and ultraviolet-visible) among the physical properties of a compound. A compound's spectra *do not vary* from one pure sample to another.

Phase Diagrams

The intermolecular forces cause compounds to exist in specific states of matter depending on the conditions; therefore, the intramolecular forces control both the melting points and boiling points of compounds.

- Solid matter is not compressible nor does it flow; the individual molecules vibrate but do not change position. In crystalline solids, the structure is regular and determined by the crystal structure. In amorphous solids or glasses, the structure is irregular.

- Liquid matter is not compressible, but it can flow; the individual molecules are in constant motion. The intermolecular distances are slightly larger than in the solids, but there is no organized structure.

- Gaseous matter is compressible and can flow; the individual molecules have a lot of kinetic energy. A gas will fill all available space, and the intermolecular distances are determined by the volume.

A phase diagram, as shown in Figure 2-1, is a graphical representation of how a specific compound behaves at varying pressures and temperatures. A substance will be in the gas form at higher temperatures and lower pressures; higher pressures and lower temperatures lead to a solid, while the substance will take on a liquid state at higher temperatures and higher pressures. The dividing lines between the different phases are representations of the transitions from one phase to another. For example, the dividing line between a gas and a liquid shows the boiling point in function of temperature and pressure; in other words, it shows a high dependency of the boiling point on pressure. The dividing line between gas and solid is also highly dependent on the pressure and represents where sublimation occurs. The line between solid and liquid phases shows how the pressure has almost no influence on the melting point of a compound; the melting point is almost constant independent of the pressure.

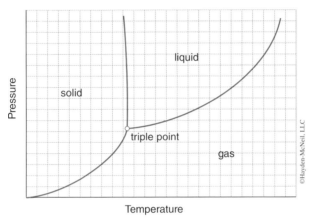

Figure 2-1. *Phase diagram.*

Melting Point for Solids

The melting point is the temperature at which the solid and liquid phases of a pure substance coexist at a pressure of 1 atmosphere (atm). At slightly higher temperature only liquid exists, while at slightly lower temperature only solid remains. The melting point of a solid is used by organic chemists to identify a compound, and also to establish its purity.

Because the presence of impurities lowers the melting point, the melting point can be a good indicator of purity: the purer the material, the higher its melting point, and the narrower the melting point range. This phenomenon is explained by the melting point behavior of mixtures. In a melting point/composition diagram, the composition of a mixture of A and B is plotted in function of its melting point, as shown in Figure 2-2. The pure substances A and B have exact melting points, T_A and T_B, respectively. But if the two are mixed, the melting point is lower in all cases. In this case, the lowest melting point is when 30 mole% A is mixed with 70 mole% B; this temperature is the eutectic point T_E. The figure also shows that if 5 mole% A is mixed with B, corresponding to 95 mole% B (almost pure), the melting point drops to T_5. This phenomenon is called "melting point depression" and gives a clear indication of the purity of a specific compound. In everyday life, this phenomenon is used when roads are salted: water and NaCl (or any other salt) form a eutectic mixture at 23 wt% NaCl, and the T_E is −21.3 °C. When salt is added to the ice on the roads, the melting point of water (0 °C) is lowered, and therefore the ice melts. The same holds true when cooling reactions in the laboratory, and even when salt and ice are mixed to make ice cream!

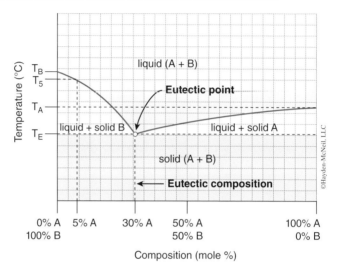

Figure 2-2. *Melting behavior of a mixture of solids.*

How Is It Done in the Lab?

A small amount of material is heated slowly and two temperatures are noted: the point at which the first liquid forms among the crystals and the point at which the whole mass of crystals turns to a clear liquid. The melting point is recorded by giving this melting point range. The sharper the range, the purer the compound.

First, get a melting point capillary with a diameter of ~1 mm. Only a small amount of solid is needed to determine its melting point; a few mg is plenty. Crush the solid on a weighing paper, and tap the open end of the capillary on the powdered solid to introduce some solid in the capillary (Figure 2-3). Invert the capillary, hold it near the bottom and tap it on a flat surface so the solid drops to the bottom of the capillary; a sample height of 1–2 mm should be sufficient. If the solid is sticky, use a long piece of straight tubing (~1 m), place it on the bench and drop the melting point capillary into the tubing. The melting point capillary will bounce a few times inside the tubing, and the solid will then collect at the bottom of the capillary. Repeat if necessary.

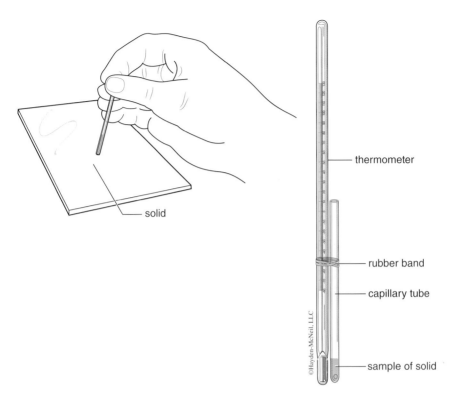

Figure 2-3. *Measurement of melting point.*

The simplest method to measure the melting point is to attach the capillary tube to a thermometer, as shown in Figure 2-3. Place an oil or water bath on a hot plate and heat; observe the solid and record the temperature at which the solid melts.

Most laboratories are equipped with Mel-Temps, which are sold under different brand names but function in the same fashion (Figure 2-4). A Mel-Temp has accurate temperature control, a thermometer, sample holders for the melting point capillaries, and a magnifying window. Both the thermometer and the sample are observed through the viewing window.

A Thiele-Dennis tube is another option (Figure 2-4). This tube contains high-boiling oil and is heated with a Bunsen burner. The oil circulates through the tube and a thermometer/melting point capillary assembly is introduced with the sample; it is held in place with a partial stopper. (You should never heat a closed vessel!) The temperature is recorded when the sample melts.

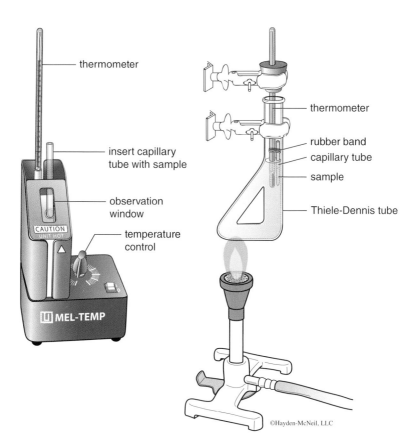

thermometer

thermometer

rubber band

insert capillary
tube with sample

capillary tube

sample

observation
window

Thiele-Dennis tube

temperature
control

CAUTION
UNIT HOT

MEL-TEMP

©Hayden-McNeil, LLC

Figure 2-4. *Melting point apparatus.*

The sample can be heated rapidly to about 20 °C below the expected melting point. From that point on, the heating rate should be very slow, about 1–2 °C per minute. Record both the temperature at which you see the first change in behavior in the solid and the temperature of complete liquefaction. This is the melting point range. If you don't know the melting point you can do a fast test run first, get a preliminary reading, and then do a very deliberate observation with a new sample.

Record the melting point in your notebook. As an example, let's use acetaminophen. This is what you would write: m.p. 166–170 °C (Lit. 169–171 °C). This observation shows a somewhat larger melting point range that is slightly lower than the literature melting point, which indicates that your sample isn't quite 100 % pure.

The main source of errors in melting point determination is heating the sample too fast—"nice and slow" is the best policy to record an accurate melting point.

A possible complication during melting point determination is decomposition of the compound, which would manifest itself by the darkening of the sample and is recorded as the temperature followed by "d" for decomposition. Sublimation is also possible before the melting point is reached, in which case the melting point capillary could be sealed before measurement.

Practical Tips

- Traces of solvent or other volatile materials can be present in a solid, which leads to "sweating" before the melting point is observed. Make sure your sample and equipment are clean and free of foreign material before beginning your experiment.

- Always start with a fresh sample for each melting point determination.

- To calibrate a melting point apparatus or a thermometer, kits of very pure standards with sharp melting points are commercially available.

- The identity of a compound can be confirmed by running a "mixed melting point." Two solids with identical melting points could be the same compound. To confirm this, grind the two solids together and record the melting point. If they are the same, the melting point does not change. If they are different compounds, melting point depression is observed.

53

Boiling Point for Volatile Liquids

Heating a liquid results in an increase of the vapor pressure of the liquid to the point where it equals the applied pressure (usually atmospheric pressure). At this point, the liquid is observed to boil. A more detailed discussion of the boiling point, and its relationship to pressure, can be found below in the section on Distillation (Chapter 3).

The normal boiling point is measured at 760 mmHg (760 torr) or 1 atm. As illustrated by the phase diagram (Figure 2-1), the liquid boils at a lower temperature at lower pressure. Because the boiling point is sensitive to pressure, it is important to record the barometric pressure when determining a boiling point if the determination is being conducted at an elevation significantly above or below sea level. Water boils at 100 °C at sea level, but in Denver (5,000 ft) it boils at 93 °C while on Mt. Everest, boiling water only reaches 72 °C. It would take a very long time to boil your eggs on top of Mt. Everest!

Just like the melting point, the boiling point is used to confirm the identity of a compound and to assess its purity.

How Is It Done in the Lab?

The boiling point can be measured during a distillation: about 5 mL of a liquid is sufficient to perform a microscale distillation (see the section on Distillation in Chapter 3).

With a smaller sample, you can use a small test tube and a (digital) thermometer. Using for example an oil bath, the liquid in the test tube is heated to reflux; the thermometer is suspended in the refluxing vapor, which gives you the boiling point (Figure 2-6). Make sure you record the atmospheric pressure as well.

For an even smaller sample, you utilize a "bell," which is a tube closed at one end and inverted, open end down, into a liquid; as the liquid is heated, the vapor pressure inside the bell will equal the external pressure on the boiling liquid (Figure 2-5). When the boiling point of the liquid is reached, bubbles form, using the rim of the bell as the nucleation point. Any liquid inside the bell is pushed out by the vapor pressure inside the bell. At the boiling point, the internal pressure (P_i) equals the external pressure (P). The heat is turned off, and as soon as the temperature is a fraction below the boiling point, the liquid will fill the capillary tube.

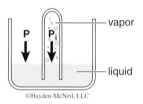

©Hayden-McNeil, LLC

Figure 2-5. *Boiling point.*

Take a TLC capillary and seal it at one end using a Bunsen burner; this will be the bell. Introduce a few drops of liquid in a melting capillary tube using a syringe with a fine needle. Place the sealed TLC capillary, open end down, inside the tube. Use a copper thread or another thin object to push the "bell" down in the liquid, and then attach the melting capillary to a thermometer as shown in Figure 2-6. Place the assembly in an oil bath; alternatively, you can use a Mel-Temp. Heat the assembly; the moment bubbles start forming at the bottom of the bell, a preliminary reading of the boiling point is taken. Take care not to overheat, or the liquid will all boil off. If the bell moves up, hold it down with the copper thread. Turn off the heat and watch the bell. The temperature at which the liquid rises inside the bell is the boiling point.

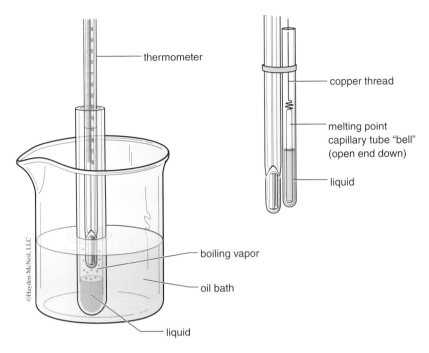

thermometer

copper thread

melting point
capillary tube "bell"
(open end down)

liquid

boiling vapor

oil bath

liquid

©Hayden-McNeil, LLC

Figure 2-6. *Boiling point determination.*

Density of Liquids

Density is defined as mass per unit volume and is generally expressed in units of grams per milliliter (g/mL) for a liquid and grams per cubic centimeter (g/cm³) for a solid. The density values for compounds are often listed in the chemical catalogs and are available from the literature.

In organic chemistry, density is most commonly used in converting the weight of liquid to a corresponding volume, or vice versa. Measuring the volume of a liquid is often easier than to weigh it. As a physical property, density is also useful for identifying liquids in much the same way that boiling points are used.

Precise methods to measure the density of liquids at the microscale level have been developed, but they are often difficult to perform. An approximate value can be determined using a 100 µL (0.100 mL) automatic pipet. Clean, dry, and pre-weigh one or more small vials and handle them with a tissue in order to avoid getting your fingerprints on them. Add 100 µL to each vial, weigh them and average the result. The units are adjusted to g/mL, and a very good approximation of the density of the liquid is obtained.

Optical Rotation (Polarimetry)

Optical activity is the ability of a compound to rotate polarized light and is directly related to the asymmetry or chirality of molecules. If a tetrahedral carbon is substituted with four different substituents, it is said to be asymmetric or chiral. Two possible configurations of this molecule exist that are mirror images of each other, just like your left and right hands are mirror images of each other. These two configurations are called enantiomers and are non-superimposable. Molecules containing these chiral carbons will rotate plane-polarized light; if a chiral molecule rotates light a certain degree to the right, then its enantiomer will rotate the light the same degree to the left. These measurements are made using a polarimeter.

Limonene is an example of a chiral molecule: one enantiomer of limonene can be found in the peels of citrus fruit, while the other one is found in pinecones (Figure 2-7). The R-isomer of limonene rotates plane-polarized light to the right, and the S-isomer rotates it to the left, as indicated by the (+) and (−) in the name. The two enantiomers have the same melting and boiling points, same behavior on TLC, and so on. So how do we differentiate the two? Besides the difference in sign of the optical rotations, we can distinguish them by their smell and taste, because most receptor sites within your body are chiral too.

Chirality plays a very important role in pharmaceuticals for the same reason: the chiral receptor sites in your body's physiology. Thalidomide is a chiral molecule which was used in the 1950s to quell morning sickness in pregnant women. Tragically, the two enantiomers had completely different effects, with the R-isomer being an effective sedative while the S-isomer caused severe birth defects estimated to have affected at least 10,000 babies, mostly in the UK. The two forms of Thalidomide interconvert at the pH in the body; so even if enantiomerically pure Thalidomide had been administered, it would still have had the same disastrous effect.

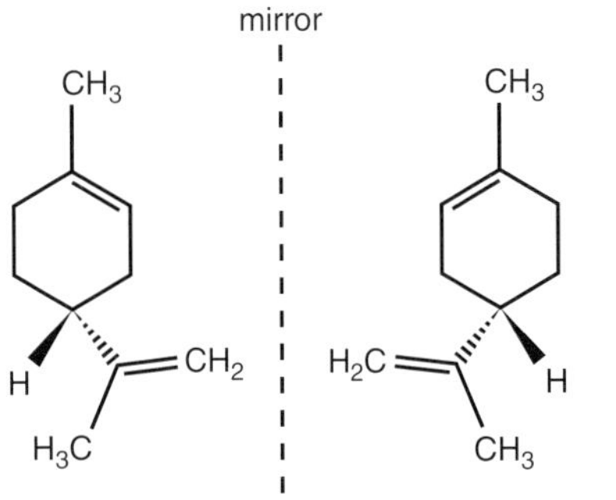

R(+)-limonene
(citrus)

$[\alpha]_D^{20} = +123°$

S(−)-limonene
(pinecones)

$[\alpha]_D^{20} = -123°$

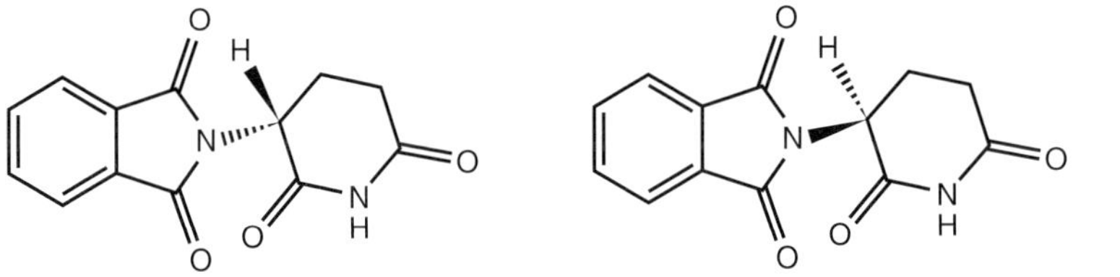

R(+)-thalidomide

S(−)-thalidomide

Figure 2-7. *Examples of chiral compounds.*

57

Optical activity is measured in a polarimeter. Ordinary white light consists of waves with a variety of wavelengths that vibrate in all possible planes perpendicular to the direction of the propagation. Light can be made monochromatic (of one wavelength of color) by using filters or special light sources. For polarimetry, a sodium lamp with a filter is used to obtain the sodium D line at 5893 angstroms. Even though this light is monochromatic, the individual light waves still vibrate in all possible planes perpendicular to the beam. A polarizing filter allows only the light which vibrates in one direction to pass through (Figure 2-8). The polarized light is then passed through a solution of an optically-active compound; this causes the polarized light to be rotated at an angle α. A second polarizing filter has to be rotated at the same angle α for the light to pass through and be observed.

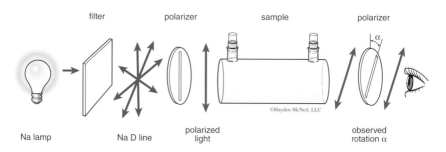

filter   polarizer   sample   polarizer

Na lamp   Na D line   polarized light   observed rotation α

©Hayden-McNeil, LLC

Figure 2-8. *Basic setup of a polarimeter.*

A polarimeter can be as simple as a lamp and two polarizing filters at each end of a container holding the compound to be measured (Figure 2 8), or as sophisticated as instruments that can cost more than \$25,000. The former requires a large sample, while dilute samples can be accurately measured with the latter.

The observed rotation α depends on the path length, the concentration of the sample and the specific rotation [α], which is an inherent property of a particular compound. As shown in Figure 2-7, the specific rotation for R-limonene is $[+123]_D^{20}$. The temperature (20 °C) and the wavelength (the Na D line) at which the measurement was made are reported. The specific rotation is calculated from the observed rotation α using the following equation:

$$\alpha = [\alpha].c.l. \quad \text{or} \quad [\alpha]_D^{20} = \frac{\alpha}{lc}$$

$[\alpha]$ = specific rotation
α = observed rotation
l = length of the sample, in dm
c = concentration of the sample, in g/mL

How Is It Done in the Lab?

A solution of the compound in question is made. Water and ethanol are very common solvents for polarimetry, but for organic compounds dichloromethane and chloroform are often used. Because α can change with solvent, both the solvent and the concentration must be specified. 10–25 mL of a solution is usually sufficient, but larger sample cells do exist. A sample cell is typically exactly 1 dm long, and is made of quartz to avoid any absorption of the light by glass. The sample cell is cylindrical and has two openings on top, as shown in Figure 2-9. These cells are very expensive and should be handled with great care.

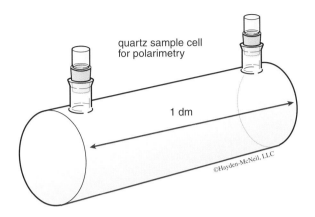

quartz sample cell
for polarimetry

1 dm

©Hayden-McNeil, LLC

Figure 2-9. *Quartz sample cell for polarimetry.*

The concentration of the solution is usually 5–10 %. Prepare the solution using a volumetric flask, and accurately report the concentration.

The sample cell must be cleaned meticulously before filling it with the solution; if possible, rinse the cell twice with a small amount of the solution. Ensure that there are no suspended particles in the solution and no air bubbles in the cell, as they will refract the light and affect the measurement. Allow enough time for the temperature of the sample to stabilize.

The polarimeter is calibrated by using pure solvent and adjusting the zero point. As it is easier to observe the absence of light, the rotation is measured at the dark point and the observed rotation α is read on the dial. If you are using an automatic polarimeter, follow the instrument instructions.

The specific rotation [α] can be calculated from one measurement. If you are comparing the optical activity of several samples, it is important to measure each sample exactly at the same concentration in the same solvent.

Enantiomeric Excess or Optical Purity

A sample of one enantiomer isolated by a resolution method or prepared synthetically is not always 100 % optically pure. Frequently, it can be contaminated by residual amounts of the opposite stereoisomer. Chemists generally use the term enantiomeric excess (ee) rather than optical purity. Enantiomeric excess is calculated using the following formula:

$$\%ee = \frac{[\alpha]_{observed}}{[\alpha]_{pure}} \times 100\ \%$$

A "pure" sample of R-limonene isolated from oranges has a specific rotation of 111, while pure limonene has a $[\alpha]$ of 123. The enantiomeric excess in this case equals

$$\%ee = \frac{111}{123} \times 100\ \% = 90.24\ \%$$

What does this mean? You have an enantiomeric excess of ~90 % R-limonene, so 10 out of every 100 molecules result in zero optical rotation. These 10 molecules are equally R- and S-limonene molecules; therefore, you have 95 R-limonene molecules for every 5 S-limonene, or 95 % optically pure R-limonene.

Refractive Index

The refractive index, n, is defined as the ratio of the velocity of light in air to the velocity of light in the medium being measured, and is another unique physical property of a chemical. The refractive index is based on the fact that light travels at a different velocity in condensed phases (e.g., liquids and solids) than in air. The refractive index can be used to characterize a pure organic compound and to assess its purity, or even to determine the composition of mixtures.

The refractive index for a given medium depends on two variable factors. First, it is temperature-dependent. The density of the medium changes with temperature; hence, the speed of light in the medium also changes. Second, the refractive index is wavelength-dependent. Beams of light with different wavelengths are refracted to different extents in the same medium and give different refractive indices for that medium.

The effect of refractive index is seen in real life when you put a fishnet under the water in an aquarium; the pole seems to bend at the point where it enters the water, which is due to the different refractive indices of air and water. The same effect makes it difficult to pick up a toy at the bottom of a swimming pool; it never is exactly where you think it is—unless you put your head under water!

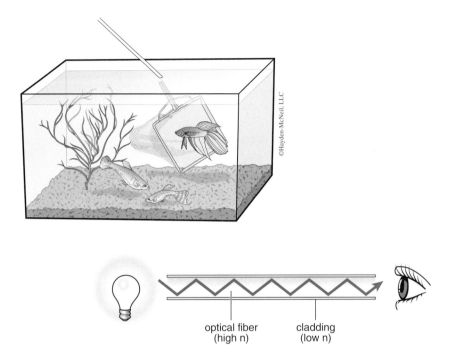

optical fiber
(high n)

cladding
(low n)

Figure 2-10. *Examples of the effect of refractive indices.*

The principles of refractive indices are applied in the construction of optical fibers. Because photons travel faster than electrons, optical fibers find more and more applications in modern telecommunication. Optical fibers are also used to provide light in otherwise inaccessible places. An optical fiber consists of a core with a high refractive index, surrounded by a cladding that has a lower refractive index. When light is sent through the fiber, it will reflect off the sides of the high refractive index core and stay contained within the core. The larger the difference in refractive index between the core and the cladding, the more efficiently the light will be transmitted through the fiber, resulting in minimal loss in signal strength. In plastic optical fibers, the core is often poly(methyl methacrylate); the cladding can be a silicone-based material, which also protects the core.

How Is It Done in the Lab?

The instrument used to measure a refractive index is a refractometer. The refractive index is dependent on temperature and wavelength, and the refractometer may have a built-in thermometer. The most commonly used refractometer is an Abbé refractometer; a typical instrument is shown in Figure 2-11. As for the light, the Na D-line is used (the same wavelength as in a polarimeter). The refractometer can be kept at exactly 20 °C by pumping water through the sample block if very exact measurements are necessary; in most cases, the temperature is noted and the refractive index at 20 °C can be calculated (see below).

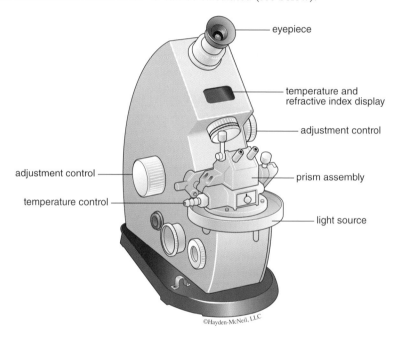

©Hayden-McNeil, LLC

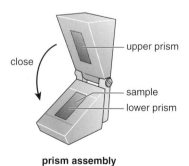

prism assembly

Figure 2-11. *Refractometer.*

The quartz prisms must be clean. If they are not, rinse with a few drops of dichloromethane or another volatile solvent and blot the surface dry with soft tissue paper. Do not rub; these quartz surfaces must not be scratched.

Place a few drops of the liquid to be measured on the lower prism, being careful not to scratch the surface, and carefully close the prism assembly. Most instruments have a locking device to ensure that the prisms are in perfect alignment.

Look through the eyepiece and turn the adjustment knobs. You should see a split optical field—dark on the bottom, light on top. Turn the knobs to achieve a sharp separation line between dark and light, and this line must be in the middle of the cross hairs. You can then either read off the refractive index below this display, or on an external read-out. In Figure 2-12, the reading is n = 1.3684. Carefully clean the prisms with soft tissue paper, again without rubbing.

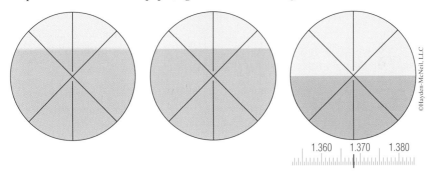

Figure 2-12. *Reading a refractive index (reading n = 1.3684).*

Practical Tips

- To calculate an accurate refractive index, you must make a temperature correction for measurements above 20 °C. For organic compounds, the refractive index decreases by 0.00045 for each degree Celsius over 20 °C.

$$n_D^{20} = n_D^{20 + x} + x(0.00045)$$

If the measurement above was done at 26 °C, the corrected value for n is

$$n_D^{20} = 1.3684 + (6 \times 0.00045) = 1.3711$$

- If your sample is volatile, you must do your measurement very quickly. It may take several tries to get an accurate reading before the sample evaporates.

- Do NOT touch the prisms with anything sharp, such as a Pasteur pipet, syringe, or spatula. Remember: only use soft tissue to clean the prism and do not rub.

• The concentration of a solution can be determined using refractive index readings. For example, this method is routinely used in the wine industry to determine the sucrose content of the wine. A calibration curve is constructed using standard samples, then the concentration of the unknown solution is determined using the refractive index.

Elemental Analysis (Molecular Formula)

Elemental analysis is a method to determine the amount, typically a weight percent, of an element in a compound. Just as there are many different elements, there are many different experiments for determining elemental composition. The most common type of elemental analysis is for carbon, hydrogen, and nitrogen (CHN analysis). This type of analysis is especially useful for organic compounds and is performed by specialized vendors. The compound to be analyzed is burned, and the amount of generated CO_2, H_2O, and nitrogen oxides is measured. With modern instrumentation only mg quantities or less compound are needed to obtain an accurate elemental analysis.

The elemental analysis of a compound is used to determine the empirical formula of a compound; this is the formula that contains the smallest set integer ratios for the elements in the compound corresponding to the elemental composition by mass.

The elemental analysis results for a specific compound read: 62.10 % C, 10.42 % H, and 0.02 % N, so we know that this compound contains carbon and hydrogen, but no nitrogen. The remainder is assumed to be oxygen, which cannot be measured using this method. Dividing the percentages of each element by the atomic weight of that element leads to the atomic ratio of each element in this molecule. For example:

$$\#C = 62.06/12 = 5.17$$

$$\#H = 10.35/1 = 10.35$$

$$\#O = 27.55/16 = 1.72$$

Dividing these numbers by the smallest number gives the molecular formula (MF) with the smallest set of integer ratios. The ratio of C/H/O is 3.04/6.017/1, which roughly corresponds to 3 C/6 H/1 O. This means that the MF for this compound could be C_3H_6O, or $C_6H_{12}O_2$, and so on. Other physical and spectroscopic measurements help decide if the compound is acetone, or oxetane, or dimethyldioxane, or even poly(oxytrimethylene) $-[-CH_2CH_2CH_2O-]_{n-}$.

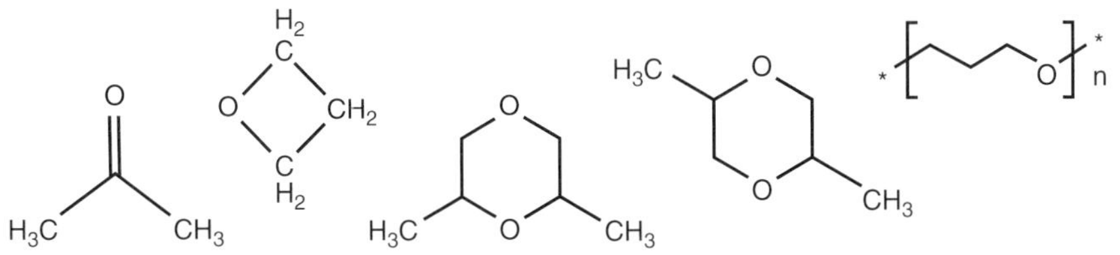

Figure 2-13. *Some examples of structures with $(C_3H_6O)_n$ molecular formula.*

Spectroscopy Introduction

The physical constants described above give information about different compounds. But unless you have literature data or have made the compound before, the fact that, for example, the melting point of a compound is 78.3 °C won't tell you anything about the structure of the compound.

Spectroscopic methods, on the other hand, give you real information about a compound's structure. Spectroscopy involves interactions of molecules with energy—light—at different wavelengths. In its simplest form, spectroscopy entails shining light on or through a sample and recording the changes in light intensity. Light is energy, and different wavelengths correspond to different energies. Therefore, different facets of the molecules can be probed and specific information about the structure acquired.

The electromagnetic spectrum ranges from the highly energetic γ-rays to radio waves with very low energy. The units are expressed in either wavelength or in frequency, depending on which "light" the chemist is dealing with; which unit is used depends on custom. Wavelength λ and frequency ν are reciprocal values, related to the speed of light, c, and they are both related to energy by Planck's equation.

$$\varepsilon = h\nu = \frac{hc}{\lambda}$$

with ε being the energy of 1 photon (1 quantum)
h is Planck's constant (6.62×10^{-34} J.s)
λ being the wavelength, the distance between one wave's maximum and the next, expressed in m or nm
ν being the frequency, the number of wave maxima per unit time, expressed in s^{-1} or hertz ($1\ Hz = 1\ s^{-1}$)
c being the speed of light, equal to 3×10^8 m/s.

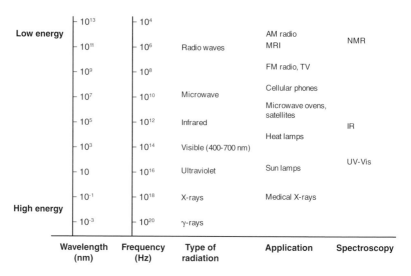

Wavelength (nm)	Frequency (Hz)	Type of radiation	Application	Spectroscopy
10^{13} **Low energy**	10^4			
10^{11}	10^6	Radio waves	AM radio MRI	NMR
10^9	10^8		FM radio, TV	
10^7	10^{10}	Microwave	Cellular phones	
10^5	10^{12}	Infrared	Microwave ovens, satellites	IR
10^3	10^{14}	Visible (400-700 nm)	Heat lamps	
10	10^{16}	Ultraviolet	Sun lamps	UV-Vis
10^{-1}	10^{18}	X-rays	Medical X-rays	
10^{-3} **High energy**	10^{20}	γ-rays		

Figure 2-14. *Electromagnetic spectrum and its applications.*

As the frequency of light varies, so does the related energy. In this context the term "light" is being used in a very broad sense. Some real-life applications of these waves are included in Figure 2-14. For example, UV light is used in sun lamps, and these are the same waves used in UV-visible spectrophotometry. NMR spectrometry—as well as magnetic resonance imaging (MRIs) in hospitals—uses radio frequency, the same energy range detected by radio antennas.

Infrared Spectroscopy

The Basic Principles

Infrared spectroscopy (IR) for organic molecules uses the wavelength region from 2.5×10^{-4} cm to 2.5×10^{-3} cm. For IR spectra, the position of the signals is expressed in wavenumbers. The wavenumber $\bar{\nu}$ is the reciprocal of the wavelength in centimeters, and therefore is expressed in cm^{-1}.

$$\text{wavenumber} = \bar{\nu} = \frac{1}{\lambda}$$

The useful IR region is from 4,000 to 400 cm^{-1}, expressed in wavenumbers $\bar{\nu}$.

When organic molecules absorb radiant energy in the IR region, specific bonds within the molecule become excited and vibrate. If the frequency of the incident radiation matches the specific vibrational frequency of the bond, the bond is excited to a higher vibrational state and the amplitude of the vibration increases.

Structurally different molecules do not absorb exactly the same energies of infrared radiation; therefore, they give differing patterns of absorption.

When absorbed, IR waves affect the vibrational modes of molecules. As shown in Figure 2-15, a tetrahedron can bend in different ways: the bonds can stretch either symmetrically or asymmetrically, but they can also bend in and out of the plane. All these movements require different energies and therefore result in different absorption signals in the IR spectrum.

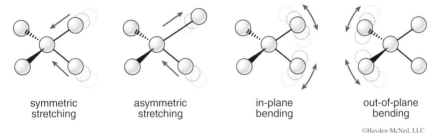

symmetric stretching · asymmetric stretching · in-plane bending · out-of-plane bending

©Hayden-McNeil, LLC

Figure 2-15. *Possible molecular vibrations.*

The Instrument

In classical dispersive spectrophotometers (Figure 2-16), the IR light is separated into different frequencies using a prism or grating. After passing through the sample, the light is sent to a detector. The spectrum is scanned one frequency at a time, and the absorption is measured.

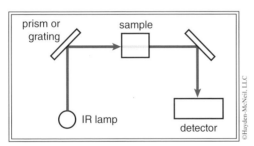

prism or grating · sample · IR lamp · detector

©Hayden-McNeil, LLC

Figure 2-16. *Basic IR spectrophotometer.*

In Fourier Transform Infrared Spectrophotometer (FTIRs), the whole spectrum is obtained at once. Fourier Transform is a mathematical algorithm used to convert the information obtained by the detector into a conventional spectrum. Fast computers scan the entire spectrum several times (usually 8 or 16 scans) in a very short period and then average the total spectrum, thus increasing the signal-to-noise ratio significantly.

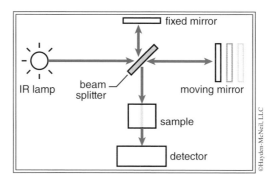

Figure 2-17. *Basic setup of FTIR.*

The key component in an FTIR is the Michelson interferometer, which modulates each wavelength of IR light at a different frequency. In an interferometer the light beam strikes a beam splitter, and about half of the light is reflected from the beam splitter and directed onto the fixed mirror. The remainder of the light is directed onto the moving mirror. When the beams combine, constructive or destructive interference occurs, depending on the position of the moving mirror relative to the fixed mirror. When both mirrors are the same distance from the beam splitter, the two reflected beams pass through exactly the same path length and consequently are totally in phase. The resulting signal intensity is at its maximum.

The modulated beam is reflected from the mirrors to the sample, where selective absorption takes place. From the sample the beam travels on to the detector, which translates the beam into an electrical signal. The interferogram is a summation of all the IR light frequencies, but it cannot be interpreted in its original form. It is converted into an IR spectrum through a Fourier Transform. The FT calculates the amplitude of each of the component signals, and the amplitude gives the intensity at the corresponding wavelength of light.

An FTIR instrument includes a laser, so caution should be used when looking inside the instrument when the cover is off. Because it emits light at a known and constant frequency, the laser acts as the internal calibrator, controls the moving mirror's position and triggers the capture of data.

The Sample

To run an infrared spectrum, place the compound in the path of the IR beam using a sample holder or cell. Because compounds with covalent bonds usually absorb, materials such as glass, quartz, and plastics absorb intensely in the infrared region of the spectrum, and they cannot be used to construct sample cells. Ionic substances on the other hand do not absorb; therefore, metal halides (sodium chloride, potassium bromide, silver chloride) are commonly used for this purpose. Using salts in cell construction, however, is not completely trivial.

For liquid samples, a common procedure is to place a drop of the liquid between two salt plates. NaCl (absorbs below 600 cm^{-1}), KBr (somewhat expensive, breaks easily), and AgCl (light sensitive, turns purple) are available commercially, and all these plates are optically clear and brittle.

For solids, the common method of sample preparation is KBr pellets. In this method, the sample is ground up with solid KBr and pressed into a thin pellet using either a press or a sample holder with two screws, as shown in Figure 2-18. The latter method is the least expensive, but it takes some practice.

A solid sample can also be ground up with Nujol, a mineral oil with minimal IR bands. The resulting mull is then pressed between two salt plates to record the spectrum.

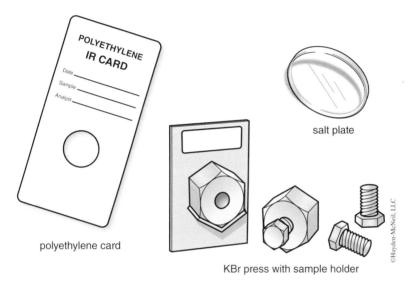

polyethylene card

KBr press with sample holder

salt plate

©Hayden-McNeil, LLC

Figure 2-18. *Sample options for IR.*

IR cards are a newer alternative (Figure 2-18). These cards contain a film of polyethylene $-(CH_2CH_2)_{n-}$ (Figure 2-19) or of Teflon $-(CF_2CF_2)_{n-}$ (Figure 2-20) onto which the sample is deposited. As can be seen in the figures, these polymers have very few peaks in the IR spectrum and therefore these peaks can be easily subtracted from the sample's spectrum. For liquids, apply 1 drop of the sample to the middle portion of the exposed film. For solids, dissolve a spatula tip of sample in about 10 drops of dichloromethane. With a pipet, place three drops of your solution on the film—the dichloromethane will evaporate very fast. Then place the "dry" card in the infrared beam and record the spectrum. In the event that a compound is not soluble in dichloromethane, another volatile solvent, such as acetone, can be used.

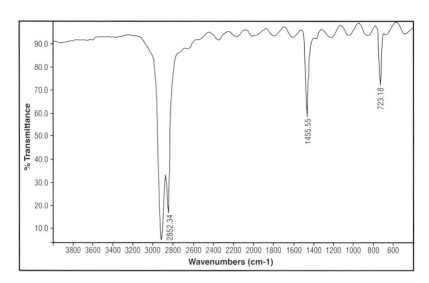

Figure 2-19. *Blank spectrum of a polyethylene film.*

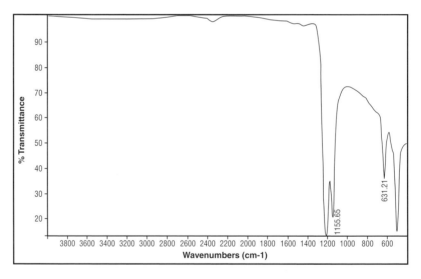

Figure 2-20. *Blank spectrum of a teflon film.*

The film can be cleaned by placing the card on a piece of tissue paper and pipetting ~10 drops of dichloromethane (or acetone) on the film to rinse it. Make sure the solvent has evaporated before reusing the card.

The Spectrum

IR spectra are usually recorded from 4,000 to 400 cm^{-1} in transmittance mode; alternatively, the signals can be displayed in absorbance mode. The portion of the spectrum between 1,500 and 400 cm^{-1} is called the fingerprint region. It acts as a human fingerprint; the pattern of the peaks is specific to a compound. A positive identification of a compound is made if the fingerprint region matches the literature IR spectrum.

Structural information is obtained from IR spectra, because functional groups have specific absorptions. The C=O group, for example, always has a strong peak in the 1600–1800 cm^{-1} region so if you see a peak in that area, it means the compound has a carbonyl functionality. Table 2-1 shows approximate values for the characteristic absorptions for functional groups.

The same information is also represented in a more visual manner in Figure 2-21, in which the regions of specific signals are indicated.

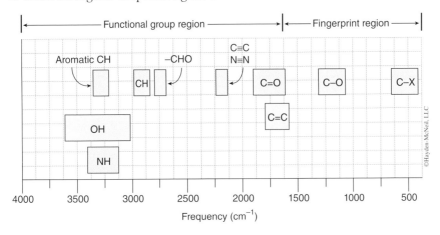

Figure 2-21. *Basic IR absorptions of functional groups.*

Table 2-1. Approximate IR Absorptions of Functional Groups

Main Functional Group	Specific Functional Group	Signal Position (cm⁻¹)	Intensity of Signal
Carbonyl C=O	Ketone R–CO–R′	1690–1715	Strong
	Aldehyde R–CHO C–H aldehydes	1680–1725 2850	Strong Weak
	Carboxylic acid – COOH	1710–1760	Strong
	Carboxylate –COO–	1610–1550 and 1400	Strong
	Ester –COOR	1720–1735	Strong
	Anhydride –CO–O–CO–	~1820 and ~1760	Strong
	Acid halide R–CO–Cl	1800	Strong
	Amide R–CO–NH₂	1650–1690	Strong
Alkene C=C	C=C Phenyl group	1645–1670 1600,1500	Weak to medium 2 sharp peaks
Alkanes C–H	C–H –CH₃	2850–3100 ~1380	Strong Sharp
Aromatic C–H		~3030 (several)	Weak
Triple Bonds	–C≡C– –C≡N	2100–2260 2210–2260	Very sharp Very sharp
Hydroxy–OH	R–OH RCO–OH	3500–3600 2500–3300	Strong Strong, very broad
Amines–NH₂	R–NH₂ R–NH–R′	3400–3500 1640–1560 3310–3350 1490–1580	Strong to medium Weak
Nitro C–NO₂	C–NO₂	1560 and 1350	Strong
Ether C–O–C	C–O–C	1050–1275	Strong
Halides C–X	C–Cl C–Br C–I	600–800 500–600 500	Strong Strong Strong

How to Interpret an IR Spectrum

The signals in an IR spectrum are characteristic of specific functional groups. IR is used to confirm the identity of a compound, as well as to help in the elucidation of the structure of an unknown. The process of analyzing the spectrum is always essentially the same. As mentioned above, the spectrum can be divided into two parts: 4000–1500 cm^{-1} will give information about functional groups and 1500–400 cm^{-1} is the fingerprint region.

When analyzing the functional group region, consider this possible practical approach to analyze the signals:

Is a carbonyl group present? (strong peak 1600–1850 cm^{-1} region)	
If YES and	If NO and
• Very broad peak for OH (3500–2000 cm^{-1}) and C=O at ~1700 cm^{-1}: *carboxylic acid* RCOOH	• Strong peak for OH at ~3500 cm^{-1}: *alcohol* ROH
• Strong peak(s) for NH (3300–3500 cm^{-1}) and C=O at ~1650 cm^{-1}: *amides* R-CO-N	• Strong peak for OH at ~3500 cm^{-1} and C=C at 1600 cm^{-1}: *phenol*
• C=O at ~1735 cm^{-1} and strong peak at ~1200 cm^{-1}: *carboxylic ester*	• Strong peak(s) for NH (3300–3500 cm^{-1}): *amine*
• Two strong C=O peaks at 1750–1850 cm^{-1}: *anhydride*	• Strong peak ~1200 cm^{-1}: *ether*
• C=O at 1800 cm^{-1} and C–Cl (600–800 cm^{-1}): *acid chloride* R–CO–Cl	• C=C at 1600 cm^{-1} and C–H at 3300 cm^{-1}: *aromatic group*
• C=O at ~1700 cm^{-1} and C–H at ~2800 cm^{-1}: *aldehyde* R–CHO	• Weak peaks at ~1650 cm^{-1}: *alkene*
• If only C=O at ~1700 cm^{-1}: *ketone*	• Sharp peak at ~2200 cm^{-1}: *acetylene or nitrile*
	• Strong peak below 600 cm^{-1}: *halide*
	• Strong peaks at 1560 and 1350 cm^{-1}: *nitro*
	• If no other peaks: *alkane*

To gain information from the fingerprint region, an authentic spectrum of your sample is recorded and compared with literature data. Many authentic spectra can be found in the literature, either in journals or in a collection of spectra, such as *The Aldrich Library of FT-IR Spectra*, *Sadtler Index*, or an online database such as the Spectral Database for Organic Compounds (Japan).

Practical Tips

- Don't try to interpret every peak. Concentrate on the important functional group peaks.

- Be aware that water is often present. A peak in the 3200–3600 cm^{-1} region does not necessarily mean that you have an OH; your sample could just have absorbed a little water.

- Think about which peaks your "sample holder" might contain. When using a polyethylene card, the spectrum can display some residual polyethylene peaks even if you ran a blank against polyethylene.

- Air can also cause peaks, most notably CO_2 and ambient water. Carbon dioxide results in a doublet at 2360 cm^{-1}, while water has a broad peak at 3600 cm^{-1} and irregular peaks at 1600 cm^{-1} due to overtones. Repeat the background spectrum if these peaks start appearing in your spectra.

- If the peaks are flat at the bottom, the sample is too concentrated. If the peaks are too weak, the sample is not concentrated enough. In either case, the spectrum must be re-run.

- Accurate wavenumber readings for peaks can be obtained with modern IR instruments. Make sure that the obtained reading refers to the maximum of the peak.

- When comparing fingerprint regions, pay close attention to the scale of the spectra. Different instruments have varying scales in different areas of the spectra.

Some Representative IR Spectra

3-Pentanone: the spectrum is shown in Figure 2-22. First, check for a carbonyl peak in the 1600–1900 cm^{-1} region; in this case, there is a peak at 1715, which could be a ketone, aldehyde, or ester. No C–H aldehyde peak is observed at 2850, nor are any strong C–O peaks observed in the 1250 cm^{-1} region, and there are no OH bands. Therefore, this spectrum is consistent with 3-pentanone. The sharp peak at 1365 corresponds to a methyl group.

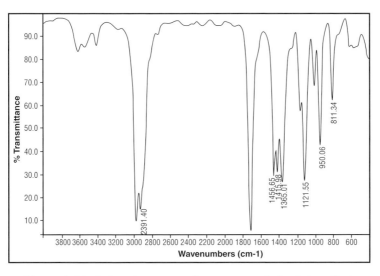

Figure 2-22. *Infrared spectrum of 3-pentanone (polyethylene film).*

1-Pentanol: The spectrum in Figure 2-23 was recorded using a polyethylene film. There are no carbonyl peaks in this sample, but the OH is very prominent at 3331 cm⁻¹. Strong C–H peaks are observed at ~3000 cm⁻¹ and the fingerprint region is consistent with the literature spectrum of 1-pentanol.

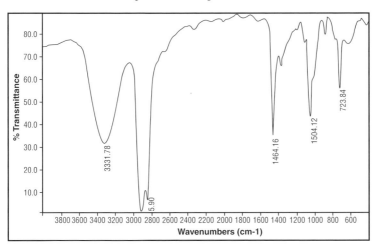

Figure 2-23. *IR Spectrum of 1-pentanol (polyethylene film).*

Resorcinol (1,3-dihydroxybenzene): The spectrum in Figure 2-24 is clearly an alcohol (strong peak observed at 3300) and has no carbonyl peak. The sharp peaks associated with an aromatic system are clearly visible at 1600 and 1485 cm⁻¹, and a weak signal at 2918 is noted for the aromatic C–H stretch.

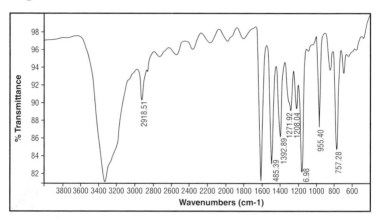

Figure 2-24. *IR Spectrum of resorcinol.*

Acetanilide C₆H₅NH–CO–CH₃: Figure 2-25 shows a clear carbonyl peak at 1657 cm⁻¹; only amides have a carbonyl peak at such low wavenumber, a fact which is confirmed by the presence of an NH peak at 3288. The sharp aromatic C=C peaks can again be noticed at 1600 and 1496. This sample is not pure, and seems to be contaminated with a carboxylic acid; the very broad OH peak is clearly visible overlapping with the NH peak. This could be due to some decomposition and possibly the presence of some acetic acid.

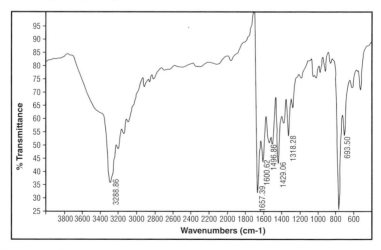

Figure 2-25. *IR spectrum of acetanilide possibly contaminated with acetic acid. The negative peak at ~ 1700 cm⁻¹ is due to incomplete background correction.*

NMR

The Basic Principles

Nuclear magnetic resonance (NMR) spectroscopy is the most widely-used technique for characterization of structure in organic chemistry, because it reveals specific placement and connectivity of atoms. While infrared spectroscopy is used to determine which functional groups are present in a molecule, NMR spectroscopy can help determine the exact location of functional groups and hydrogens. NMR spectroscopy gives valuable information about the carbon skeleton and about the molecule as a whole.

NMR spectroscopy can be applied for any nucleus that has a nuclear spin; that is, any nucleus that has an odd mass number and/or odd atomic number. The most common type of NMR is ^{1}H (proton) NMR, and the use of ^{13}C NMR is also widespread. For ^{1}H NMR, the chemist is relying on the most abundant isotope of hydrogen, while in the case of ^{13}C NMR the ^{13}C isotope only represents roughly 1 % of the carbon atoms.

In NMR the nucleus is observed. Consider the nucleus as a tiny magnet that is positively charged. The nucleus spins and, if placed in a strong magnetic field, the spin aligns with the magnetic field and precesses very much like a child's top (Figure 2-26). The spin for ^{1}H is $+\frac{1}{2}$ and, though aligned with the magnetic field, the nucleus rotates at an angle.

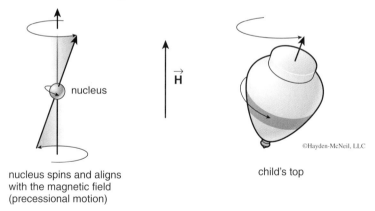

nucleus

$\vec{H}$

©Hayden-McNeil, LLC

nucleus spins and aligns
with the magnetic field
(precessional motion)

child's top

Figure 2-26. *Effect of magnetic field on nucleus spin.*

If a radio frequency is applied, the nucleus flips to a higher energy state—against the magnetic field—and the spin is $-\frac{1}{2}$ (Figure 2-27). The difference in energy is very small and corresponds to low energy radio waves, and the protons are said to be in "resonance." When an NMR is run, a very short, powerful "ping" of radio waves is applied, which flips most spins to the higher energy state (Figure 2-28). The decay of the signal is then observed for a certain time period while the spins slowly fall back to the lower-level spin aligned with the magnetic field. This process is called free induction decay, or FID. The raw signal is an oscillating curve that is converted to an NMR spectrum using the mathematical function Fourier Transform.

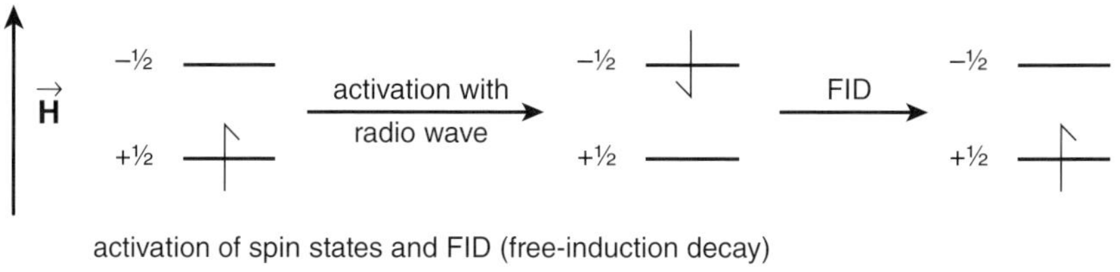

Figure 2-27. *Effect of radio wave on nucleus spin.*

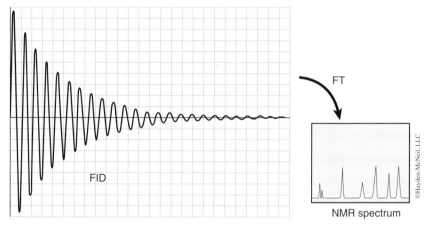

The FID signal is converted using Fourier Transform to a conventional NMR spectrum.

Figure 2-28. *Free induction decay in NMR.*

In ¹H-NMR the hydrogen nucleus, a proton, is observed, and the terms hydrogen and proton are used interchangeably in NMR. This is somewhat different from the way a proton is considered in a reaction mechanism when a proton specifically refers to H^+, which after all is actually a hydrogen nucleus!

The Instrument

A nuclear magnetic resonance spectrometer consists of a magnet, in which the sample is placed. The magnet is very powerful (>1 Tesla), and objects that might be affected by the magnetic field, such as credit cards, should not be brought into the NMR room, nor should people with pacemakers enter these rooms.

The high magnetic fields are achieved using a superconducting magnet, a Nb/Ti alloy, which is cooled in liquid He (4 K). The liquid He container is surrounded by a liquid nitrogen container, to help maintain the low temperature. The probe is equipped with a radio transmitter and a receiver, connected through an amplifier to a computer for data processing (Figure 2-29). The sample in the NMR tube is "dropped" into the probe and spins very rapidly. NMR tubes are quite narrow, 5 mm diameter, and rather long (~7–20 cm).

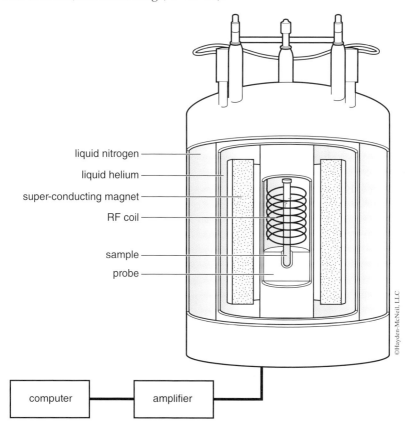

Figure 2-29. *Basic setup of NMR instrument.*

The strength of a particular NMR instrument is indicated by its operating frequency, meaning the frequency at which the nuclei resonate. Older ¹H instruments are 60 MHz, which is the radio frequency used for protons in this specific magnet. Newer more powerful instruments range from 200 to 600 MHz, and even 800 MHz. The higher frequencies lead to more detailed spectra, and therefore more information. Comparing the two ¹H spectra of m-isopropoxytoluene recorded at 60 MHz and 300 MHz, the difference between the two spectra is obvious. The 300 MHz spectrum shows much more detail, but at first sight the peaks are "crunched" together. A blow-up of the area at δ 4.5 shows the detail of the spectrum; also notice the much cleaner peaks around δ 7.0, which correspond to the aromatic protons.

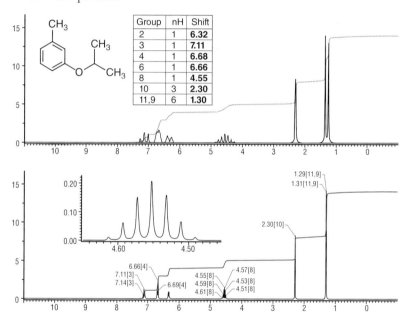

Figure 2-30. *NMR Spectra of* m-*Isopropoxytoluene, at 60 MHz (top spectrum) and at 300 MHz (bottom, with detailed insert).*

For ¹³C, the resonant frequency is different from the proton at the specific magnetic field; the ¹³C resonant frequency is roughly ¼ of the ¹H frequency. Thus, for a magnet with a field strength of 7 Tesla, the ¹H resonant frequency is 300 MHz, while the ¹³C resonant frequency is roughly 75 MHz. ¹³C NMR will be discussed in further detail below.

The Sample

NMR spectra are usually run in dilute solutions. An NMR tube is a long, very thin tube, as shown in Figure 2-31; the tube has a diameter of ~5 mm. The NMR tube must be scrupulously clean before use. A small amount of the sample is introduced; the sample size can vary from a fraction of 1 mg to 5–20 mg. The sample is then diluted in a solvent, up to a height of 2–4 cm, depending on the instrument used to run the sample.

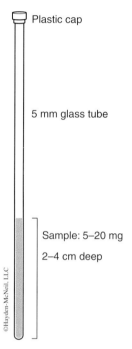

Plastic cap

5 mm glass tube

Sample: 5–20 mg

2–4 cm deep

©Hayden-McNeil, LLC

Figure 2-31. *NMR tube.*

The solvent should either not have an NMR signal at all, or at the very least have a signal that does not interfere with the spectrum being recorded. For proton NMR, solvents without protons should be used. The most common solvents are deuterated; deuterium's signal in NMR is very far removed from the proton spectra we are recording. Another reason to use a deuterated solvent is that the deuterium signal provides a "lock" for the instrument, which helps to calibrate the instrument during the consecutive scans.

Table 2-2 lists common NMR solvents, as well as those peaks that the small fraction of non-deuterated molecules would display in the spectrum. Consider the most common solvent, deuterated chloroform $CDCl_3$. Chloroform is a very good solvent for most organic compounds, and is not too expensive. Commercial $CDCl_3$ is 99.8 % deuterated, which means it still contains 0.2 % $CHCl_3$. Therefore each NMR spectrum will contain a very small peak due to the remaining $CHCl_3$, and this peak can be found at δ 7.3 ppm.

Table 2-2. Common NMR Solvents and Their NMR Signals

Solvent	Formula	NMR signal (δ, ppm)
Chloroform-d	$CDCl_3$	7.3 (s)
Acetone-d$_6$	$(CD_3)_2C{=}O$	2.1 (s)
DMSO-d$_6$	$(CD_3)_2S{=}O$	3.6 (m)
Benzene-d$_6$	C_6D_6	7.4 (s)
Deuterium oxide	D_2O	4–5 (br)
Tetrahydrofuran-d$_8$	C_4D_8O	1.9 (m), 3.8 (m)
Dichloromethane-d$_2$	CD_2Cl_2	5.2 (s)

The ¹H Spectrum

As shown in Figure 2-30, a ¹H spectrum is represented on a scale from 0 to 10. A standard is necessary, and for ¹H NMR tetramethylsilane $(CH_3)_4Si$ (TMS) is used; the TMS signal is the 0 point. Note that the peak at δ 0.0 does not appear in the spectra in this book because these are simulated spectra.

The scale of the x-axis in an NMR spectrum is expressed in ppm. Each ppm in Hz is equal to the frequency of the instrument divided by 10^6. Therefore, when using a 60 MHz (60,000,000 Hz) instrument, 1 ppm is equal to 60 Hz, while for a much more powerful 600 MHz instrument, 1 ppm equals 600 Hz. As will be shown, the latter will yield much more structural information.

The position of a peak is expressed as the chemical shift δ; δ is equal to the signal frequency in Hz divided by the instrument frequency in MHz multiplied by 10^6. In practice, δ will be on a scale from 0 to 10 or higher.

$$\delta\,(\text{ppm}) = \frac{\text{signal frequency (Hz)}}{\text{applied frequency (MHz)}} \times 10^6$$

A Simple Explanation of ¹H NMR Spectra

For a particular type of atom, such as ¹H in proton NMR, the spectrum shows peaks or signals, and from these the chemist will deduce information about the structure of the molecule. As explained above, the signal is due to the FID; we are observing the energy which is released when the spin of the nucleus flips back to realign itself with the applied magnetic field (Figures 2-27 and 2-28).

Let's start with **methane**, CH_4. If we dissolve methane in $CDCl_3$ and run an NMR, we can only observe one kind of proton; i.e., one peak. All hydrogens, or protons, in methane are equivalent, and therefore will behave exactly in the same fashion. As shown in Figure 2-32, a peak is observed at δ 0.3. The first principle of NMR is that *equivalent hydrogens result in only one signal.*

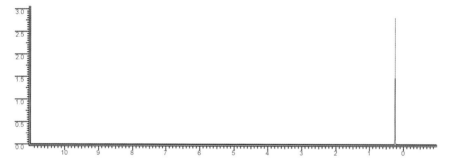

Figure 2-32. *NMR of methane CH_4 in $CDCl_3$.*

The spectrum of **ethane** CH_3CH_3 (Figure 2-33) looks very similar, again one peak, but now the chemical shift is δ 0.9; the peak shifted. The protons in ethane are very similar to the protons in methane, but not quite the same. Again we only see a singlet, a single peak, and this is consistent with the principle that all equivalent hydrogens only display one peak.

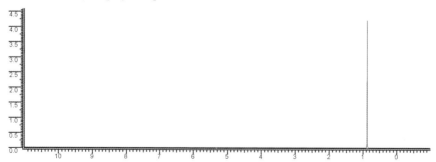

Figure 2-33. *NMR of ethane CH_3CH_3 in $CDCl_3$.*

In the NMR of **dimethyl ether** CH_3OCH_3 (Figure 2-34), notice that there is still only one peak, consistent with the rule that all equivalent hydrogens give only one signal. However, the peak has shifted quite a bit, to δ 3.0. This is because the hydrogens in dimethyl ether are in a different environment than the hydrocarbon hydrogens in methane and ethane. The hydrogens in dimethyl ether are on a carbon adjacent to the more electronegative oxygen, and the environment of the hydrogens in the molecule will influence the energy difference between the two spin states. Electronegative substituents result in a "downfield" shift, meaning a shift to higher δ. This leads us to the second principle in NMR: *The chemical shift of a peak is dependent on the molecular environment the protons are in.*

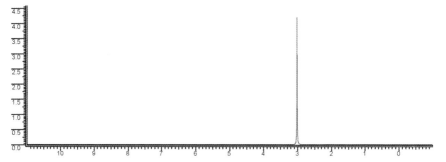

Figure 2-34. *NMR spectrum of dimethyl ether CH_3OCH_3 in $CDCl_3$.*

t-**Butyl methyl ether** $CH_3O-C(CH_3)_3$ has two kinds of protons, the nine *t*-butyl protons are rather hydrocarbon-like, while the three methoxy protons are almost exactly the same as the dimethyl ether protons. As a result, the NMR of methyl *t*-butyl ether, shown in Figure 2-35, has two peaks; one large peak at δ 1.2, corresponding to the *t*-butyl protons, and one smaller peak at δ 3.1 representing the CH_3O- protons.

The area underneath the peaks is directly proportional to the number of protons the peak represents. The computer calculates the area under the peaks by using integration, which is represented in the spectrum by the horizontal line. The area of the peaks is measured by the "rise" in this horizontal line and is directly proportional to the number of hydrogens the peak represents. In Figure 2-35, the integration of the peak at δ 3.1 is 1.91, and the peak at δ 1.2 is 5.73. The ratio 5.73/1.91 is 3, which means that one peak represents three times as many protons as the other peak. The third principle of NMR spectra, therefore, is: *The surface under the peaks, the integration, represents the relative number of protons of each type in the molecule.*

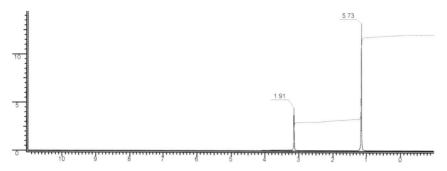

Figure 2-35. *NMR spectrum of* t-*butyl methyl ether* CH_3-O-$C(CH_3)_3$.

Diethyl ether $(CH_3CH_2)_2O$ also has two kinds of protons, but as shown in Figure 2-36 the spectrum is more complex, because the signals are split: the signal at δ 3.4 is split in four peaks (quadruplet), while the signal at δ 1.2 is split in three peaks (triplet). Consistent with the principles outlined above, the protons on the α-carbon next to oxygen are at higher chemical shift than the protons on the β-carbon, which are more hydrocarbon-like, and the integration indicates a ratio of 2 to 3, respectively.

The methyl protons (δ 1.2) are subjected to the instrument magnetic field, but they can also feel the tiny magnetic fields generated by the spinning nuclei of the methylene CH_2 group. Those spins can either be both aligned with the magnetic field, or both against, or one up and one down. The latter is twice as likely, as shown in Figure 2-37. Therefore, the methyl protons feel three different magnetic fields and yield three different peaks, with the middle one being double the size of the other two.

When the situation of the methylene protons is analyzed, there are four possibilities for the spins of the methyl protons (Figure 2-37). This will result in a quadruplet, with the inside peaks being three times as large as the outside peaks.

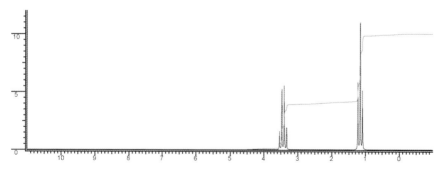

Figure 2-36. *NMR spectrum of diethyl ether* $(CH_3CH_2)_2O$.

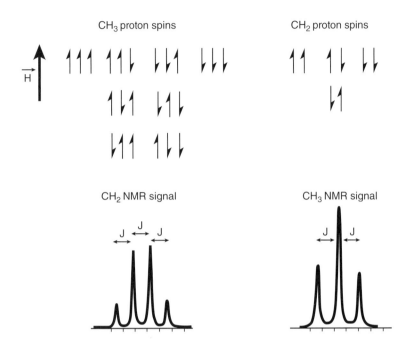

Figure 2-37. *Visualization of splitting patterns.*

The fourth principle of NMR spectra is: *The splitting or multiplicity of a signal is determined by the number of protons on the neighboring carbon plus one, n + 1.*

The distance between the peaks is determined by the coupling constant J. Notice that the coupling constants, expressed in Hz, are the same for related signals. As the quadruplet and triplet in the spectrum of diethyl ether are related, the coupling constant is the same in both multiplets, 7.0 Hz. How was this determined? The peaks in the triplet are respectively at 1.21, 1.14, and 1.08 ppm, the difference is 0.07 ppm, and as this is a spectrum recorded on a 100 MHz instrument 1 ppm = 100 Hz. Therefore, J = 0.07 ppm • 100 Hz/ppm = 7.0 Hz. The coupling constant is influenced by many factors, such as length of bonds and dihedral angles, and will be discussed below. Therefore, the fifth principle of NMR spectra is: *Coupling constants of "related" multiplets are the same.*

To summarize:

• Non-equivalent hydrogens result in different signals.

• The chemical shift is determined by the chemical environment of the protons.

• The integration corresponds to the number of equivalent protons responsible for a specific signal.

- The splitting pattern is determined by the number of protons on the neighboring carbon n: the multiplicity of a signal is n+1.

- "Related" multiplets have the same coupling constants.

Equivalent Hydrogens and Integration

Protons in the same chemical environment are said to be equivalent and will result in one signal in the NMR spectrum; it is therefore essential to be able to recognize equivalency in a chemical formula.

Each set of equivalent protons results in one signal, but this signal can be split. Therefore, it is also necessary to be able to distinguish how many types of protons are in the NMR spectrum, as this is important structural information.

The integration of the signal gives information about the number of the protons this particular signal represents. Again, the NMR spectrometer will integrate the NMR signals, which gives relative information about the number of protons.

Figure 2-38 shows different molecules and indicates how many different kinds of protons are in each. Cyclobutane, benzene, and dioxane have only one type of protons; therefore, the NMR spectrum will consist of only a singlet. The other two compounds in Figure 2-38 have two kinds of protons, so the NMR spectrum will consist of two signals. In these particular cases there are two singlets in each of these spectra, since equivalent protons do not split each other and there are no hydrogens on neighboring carbons.

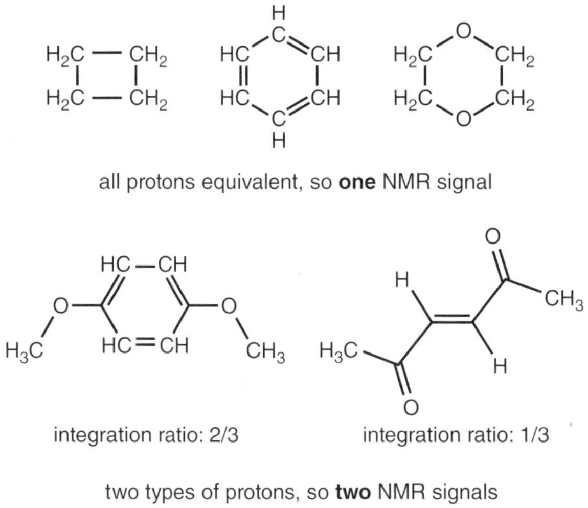

all protons equivalent, so **one** NMR signal

integration ratio: 2/3   integration ratio: 1/3

two types of protons, so **two** NMR signals

Figure 2-38. *Proton equivalence and integration.*

Looking at a more complex system, we can analyze the structure used in Figure 2-30:

Types of Protons	Integration	Splitting
CH₃ toluene	3	1
2* CH₃ isopropyl	6	2
CH isopropyl	1	7
H¹ aromatic	1	1
H² aromatic	1	2
H³ aromatic	1	2 × 2
H⁴ aromatic	1	2

There are 7 kinds of protons in this structure. In Figure 2-30, the signals of the methyl and isopropoxy groups are easily recognized, but the peaks of the aromatic protons are somewhat muddled. The lesson here is that it isn't always easy to distinguish the different types of protons in the spectrum.

The integration of the different types of protons in Figure 2-30 reveals that the ratio of the signals going from left to right is 1:2:1:1:3:6. In this case, two of the aromatic protons have roughly the same chemical shift and the signals overlap.

Chemical Shift in ¹H Spectra

One of the major advantages of NMR is that the position of the signals—the chemical shift—gives us clues about the chemical environment of the protons in question. The different areas of the spectrum correspond to certain functional groups. A representation of the different chemical shifts is shown in Figure 2-39, and the same data are collected in Table 2-3.

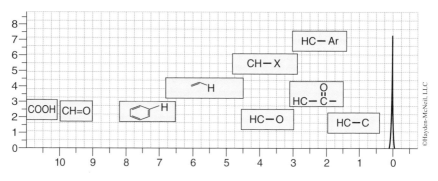

Figure 2-39. *Chemical shifts of common functional groups.*

Table 2-3. ¹H NMR Chemical Shifts

Functional Group	Proton Connectivity	Chemical Shift (δ, ppm)
Alkane	R–CH$_3$ R–CH$_2$–R′ R$_3$–CH	0.9 1.3 1.6
Halide	H–C–Br H–C–Cl H–C–F	2.5–4.0 3.1–4.1 4.2–4.8
Alcohol	CH–OH C–OH	3.4–4.0 0–5
Ether	CH–O–R	3.2–3.6
Amine	CH–NH$_2$ C–NH$_2$	2.5–3.1 0–5
Ketone	CH–C=O	2.0–2.5
Aldehyde	CH–(C=O)H CH–(C=O)H	2.2–2.4 9–10
Ester	CH–COOR C–(C=O)O–CH–R	2–2.5 3.7–5
Carboxylic acid	CH–COOR C–COOH	2.0–2.6 10–12
Alkene	HC=C HC–C=C	4.0–6.8 1.7–2.2
Aromatic	H–Phenyl CH–Phenyl	6.5–8.5 2.2–3.0

Two more comments on chemical shift:

- The effect of multiple substituents is additive. For example, a CH$_2$ next to one Cl will be at $\delta \sim 3.5$, but with two adjacent Cl substituents, as in dichloromethane, the signal has shifted to δ 5.2. Detailed tables for chemical shift can be found in the literature.

- Exchangeable protons, such as –OH and –NH$_2$ can be found in very wide regions depending on the solvent. They tend to be somewhat broader than protons on C.

Splitting

A signal will be split depending on how many protons are on the next carbon, and if there are n protons, the signal will be split into n+1 peaks. Figure 2-40 shows a few typical splitting patterns. Two adjacent methylene (CH$_2$) groups lead to two

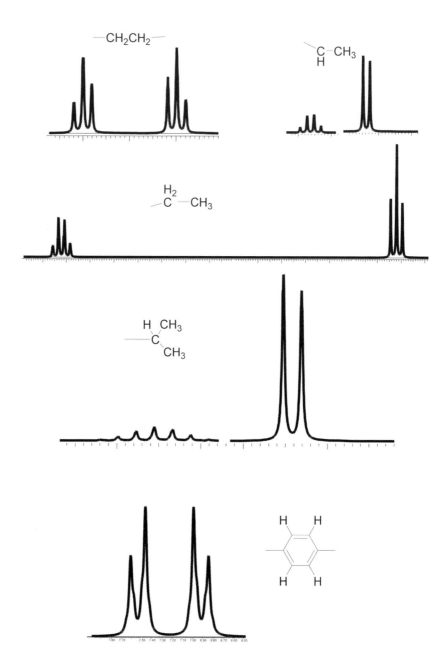

Figure 2-40. *A few typical splitting patterns.*

triplets, and a methyl next to a CH group results in a quadruplet and a doublet. An ethyl group is easily recognizable due to its quadruplet/triplet pattern, while the isopropyl group is identifiable by its large doublet along with a small multiplet (septet). A para-substituted benzene ring is clearly identified by two doublets in the δ 7–8 ppm region.

Protons between different protons will be split by both. Considering the spectrum of 1-chloropropane in Figure 2-41:

- The signal for the methyl group is at δ 1.0 and is a triplet due to the adjacent methylene.

- The methylene next to chlorine is at δ 3.5 and is also a triplet due to the adjacent methylene.

- The central methylene group (δ 1.75) is split by both the methyl and the methylene next to chlorine. The splitting is therefore $(3 + 1) \times (2 + 1) = 12$. This is a multiplet, and at the resolution in Figure 2-41 all peaks are not distinguishable.

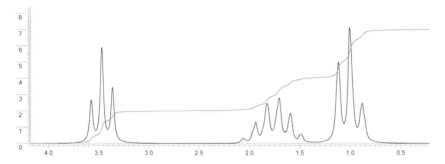

Figure 2-41. *NMR spectrum of 1-chloropropane* CH_3–CH_2–CH_2–Cl.

In this discussion, it is important to remember that equivalent protons do not split each other. Therefore, butane CH_3–CH_2–CH_2–CH_3, which has two kinds of protons, results in two signals. The signal for the methyl group is a triplet, due to the adjacent methylene group. The methylene protons are all identical and so do not split each other, so this signal is therefore split into a quadruplet as only the 3 protons of the methyl contribute to the splitting.

As mentioned above, the coupling constant J is the distance between the individual peaks in the multiplets created by the splitting and is the same for two related splitting patterns. The magnitude of J can yield information about the environment of the protons; Table 2-4 lists some typical proton-proton coupling constants. As the few listed patterns indicate, the geometric relationship of the adjacent protons has a significant influence on the J value, which can range from −12 Hz to 18 Hz, or even larger. The coupling constant of vinyl protons will clearly indicate if the protons are cis or trans on the double bond, or if they are on the same carbon. More rigid molecules can lead to more complex splitting patterns. All this information yields more details about the structure of the compounds.

Table 2-4. Proton-proton Coupling Constants (Hz)

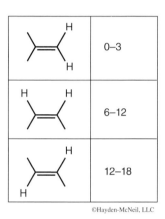

H₂C—CH	free rotation	7
H₂C—CH	syn or gauche	2–4
H₂C—C	anti	8–12
C(H)(H)	geminal	(-8)–(-12)

(vinyl, H top, two H right)	0–3
(vinyl, cis)	6–12
(vinyl, trans)	12–18

©Hayden-McNeil, LLC

How to Interpret ¹H NMR Spectra

A systematic procedure, as outlined, will help you solve the structure of compounds. If the molecular formula of the compound is known, then basic information can be deduced from this, as discussed in the section on Elemental Analysis. The main question to address is: How many unsaturations (double bonds and/or rings) does the compound have?

As for the NMR spectra itself:

- How many different kinds of protons are present? Each set of equivalent protons will lead to one signal, which might be split into several peaks.

- How many protons are represented by each signal? The integration of the peaks reveals the relative number of each kind of protons.

- Determine the chemical shift of each signal. This will indicate which kind of protons are in the compound: are they aromatic? Vinylic? An aldehyde proton? Alkane-like? And so on.

- Determine the multiplicity of each signal, which reveals how many protons are on the neighboring carbon. Patterns such as a quadruplet and a triplet, which integrate for 2 and 3 protons respectively, lead to the conclusion that an ethyl group is present in the compound. Other patterns can be deduced.

- Finally, the coupling constant will yield information about the geometric relationship of protons. For example, two vinylic protons can be either cis or trans, and the J value will indicate which one it is.

- Combine all acquired information and ensure that the data are consistent with each other.

A Few Simple Examples of ¹H NMR Spectra

Spectrum 1: A compound with molecular formula $C_6H_{12}O$ has the following NMR spectrum:

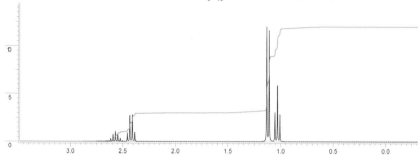

How can we deduce the structure?

• The molecular formula is used to calculate the number of unsaturations:

  #C + 1 − [(#H + #X)/2] = 6 + 1 − (12/2) = 1 unsaturation, so either 1 double bond, or 1 ring.

• There are four groups of peaks; i.e., four different kinds of protons.

• The integration has a ratio of (from left to right) 1:2:6:3.

• Two sets of peaks are at δ ~2.5, which indicates that they are next to an elec-tronegative functional group such as a halide (not in the MF) or a phenyl (not enough carbons) or a carbonyl (probably the best choice here), and the other two sets of peaks are in the hydrocarbon region.

• The multiplet at δ 2.65 could be a quintuplet or more, which means there are lots of protons on the neighboring carbons; it integrates for 1 H. This would place it next to the protons that are responsible for the doublet at δ 1.25, which integrates for 6 H; therefore, this could be an isopropyl group, -CH(CH₃)₂.

• The two other sets of peaks are a quadruplet at δ 2.3 (integration 2 H, 3 H on the next carbon) and a triplet at δ 1.05 (integration 3 H, 2 H on the next carbon).

• All this information combined leads to the correct structure: 2-methyl-3-pentanone.

Spectrum 2: MF $C_{10}H_{13}ClO$

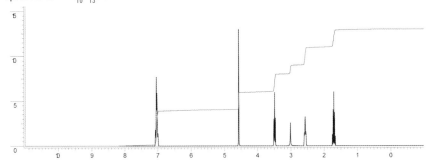

- The molecular formula is used to calculate the number of unsaturations:

  #C + 1 – [(#H + #X)/2] = 10 + 1 – (14/2) = 4 unsaturations, so either 4 double bonds, or 3 double bonds and 1 ring, and so on.

- Six kinds of protons, integration ratio 4:2:2:1:2:2.

- Signal at δ 7 ppm, aromatic protons, corresponds to 4 H, so di-substituted aromatic ring (probably para), 4 unsaturations (3 double bonds and 1 ring), which is consistent with the MF.

- 1 singlet at δ 4.6, integration 2 H, probably doubly substituted, since it is so far downfield. We know there are no more double bonds in the compound because the aromatic ring accounts for the 4 unsaturations.

- Multiplets at δ 3.5, 2.6, and 1.7, all integrate for 2 H each, which implies CH_2–CH_2–CH_2, with the multiplet at δ 1.7 being the middle methylene group (most hydrocarbon-like).

- Lonely singlet at δ 3.0 is somewhat broader and probably due to an OH (exchangeable proton).

- Assembling all this information leads us to a phenyl ring with 2 substituents: a propylene chain and a methylene, with either Cl or OH at the end of each one.

- Note: in this case it is not possible to differentiate the two possible isomers by ¹H NMR alone.

^{13}C NMR

Carbon is another atom which can be used for NMR to elucidate the structure of organic compounds. For C NMR, we have to look at the signal of ^{13}C, because it is the C-isotope with an odd mass, and therefore a nuclear spin. The most abundant isotope of carbon, ^{12}C, is NMR inactive. One big disadvantage of having to use the ^{13}C-isotope is that its natural abundance is only 1.08 % of all carbons in nature; basically only 1 of every 100 C-atoms in a sample will be NMR active. As a consequence, the NMR signal will be much weaker. Modern Fourier transform instrumentation allows the chemist to obtain good spectra in spite of this problem. Another consequence of this low natural abundance is that the chance of one molecule containing more than one ^{13}C is negligible.

For ^{13}C NMR spectra, the zero is determined by the TMS signal, just like in ^{1}H NMR, but in this case the carbons of the methyl groups are the source of the reference signal. The chemical shifts range from 0 to 220 ppm, a much larger range than for ^{1}H NMR. The hydrocarbon-like carbons are at the lowest chemical shifts, and carbons substituted with heteroatoms are at higher chemical shifts, followed by the carbons involved in double and triple bonds and aromatic carbons. So far the sequence roughly mimics the sequence seen in the ^{1}H NMR spectra, even though the chemical shift differences are larger; the large difference is the position of the carbons of carbonyl and cyano groups, which are at the chemical shifts above 150 ppm. Table 2-5 lists chemical shift ranges for different kinds of carbons in organic molecules. More precise values for chemical shifts of carbons can be calculated using tables available in the literature and more advanced spectroscopy textbooks. Software packages like ChemDraw have the capability of calculating the ^{13}C NMR spectra of many compounds.

Table 2-5. Common Approximate Chemical Shifts in ^{13}C NMR

Functional Group	Carbon Connectivity	Chemical Shift (δ, ppm)
Alkane	R–CH$_3$ R–CH$_2$–R' R$_3$–CH	5–30 15–55 20–60
Halide	C–Br C–Cl	25–65 35–80
Alcohol, Ether, Ester rest	C–O	40–80
Amine	C–N	30–65
Alkyne	–C≡C–	65–90
Alkene	C=C	100–140
Phenyl	C—	120–160
Nitrile	–C≡N	110–140
Carbonyl	C=O	155–220

Because of the low natural abundance of ^{13}C, there is basically no chance that two NMR-active carbons will be next to each other, i.e., there is no ^{13}C–^{13}C splitting (homonuclear splitting). Because of the method used to record most ^{13}C spectra, the splitting with the neighboring proton is not observed (see below). Therefore only singlets will be observed in a ^{13}C spectrum. It is also known that equivalent carbons give the same NMR signal. As a consequence, the number of peaks in a ^{13}C spectrum corresponds to the number of non-equivalent carbons present in the sample.

On the other hand, most carbon atoms will have H-substituents, and the protons are NMR active. These protons will split the carbon signal following the n+1 rule; this is heteronuclear splitting between ^{13}C and ^{1}H, a one-bond coupling. Most ^{13}C spectra are run as proton-decoupled spectra, during which all protons are irradiated so that the ^{13}C–^{1}H coupling disappears from the spectrum. This results in the nice and simple ^{13}C NMR spectra with a singlet for each non-equivalent carbon.

A Few Examples of ¹³C NMR Spectra

Example 1:

Identify the peaks in the ¹³C spectrum of *p*-methoxy-acetophenone.

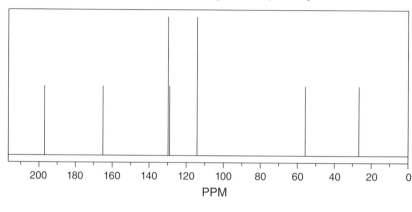

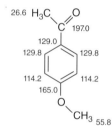

- There are seven peaks in the spectrum, while there are 9 carbons in the structure. Therefore two pairs of carbons have to be equivalent: symmetry indicates that the carbons ortho and meta to the carbonyl group are equivalent.

- Starting at the high chemical shift end of the spectrum, the peak at ~200 ppm is easily identified as the carbonyl carbon.

- The four peaks between 170 and 110 ppm belong to the aromatic ring: the peak at 165 ppm is next to the oxygen, the smaller peak at 129 ppm is the peak next to the carbonyl group. The other two peaks are larger in this simulated spectrum, and belong to the other carbons in the aromatic ring. As to which is which, detailed calculations, which are beyond the scope of this discussion, reveal that the ortho carbons to carbonyl are at ~130 ppm, while the ones at 114 ppm are the meta carbons.

- The peak at 56 ppm is the methyl carbon in the methoxy group (larger effect than carbonyl), while the peak at 27 ppm is the carbon next to the carbonyl group.

Example 2:

Two samples with a molecular formula $C_4H_8O_2$ have the following ^{13}C spectra:

Spectrum 1

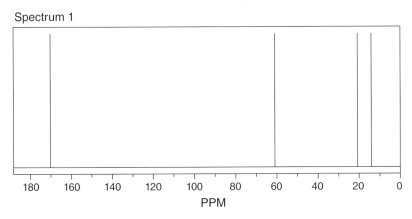

Spectrum 2

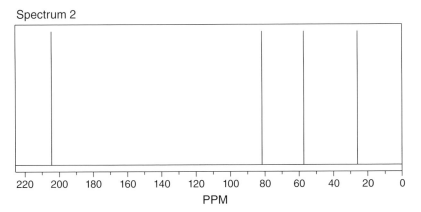

- The molecular formula is used to calculate the number of unsaturations:

  #C + 1 − [(#H + #X)/2] = 4 + 1 − 4 = 1 unsaturation, so either a double bond or a ring.

- The peaks at δ 170 ppm and at δ 205 ppm in these two spectra are clear indications of the presence of a carbonyl group in both compounds.

- There are 4 peaks in each spectrum, therefore there are no equivalent carbons in these compounds.

- Spectrum 1 has two peaks below 20 ppm, an indication of hydrocarbon character, while the third carbon is at ~60 ppm, so possibly next to an oxygen.

- All signals are at higher chemical shifts in Spectrum 2, indicating that all carbons are next to a functionality.

- Using this MF and knowing that there is a carbonyl in both molecules, there are only two possible isomers, ethyl acetate and 4-oxa-2-pentanone:

- The peaks and compounds can be assigned as follows:

Spectrum 1: Ethyl acetate	δ (ppm): 15 (CH$_3$ in ethyl group), 21 (CH$_3$ next to carbonyl), 61 (CH$_2$ next to O), 170 (carbonyl)
Spectrum 2: 4-Oxa-2-pentanone	δ (ppm): 26 (CH$_3$ next to carbonyl), 57 (CH$_3$ next to O), 82 (CH$_2$ between carbonyl and O), 170 (carbonyl)

Other NMR Methods

NMR is clearly the most used method for identification of organic compounds, and over the years many sophisticated methods have been developed to extract more information out of NMR. A few of these methods are listed here, with a very rudimentary explanation:

- **Proton-coupled ^{13}C NMR:** In this case the protons are not irradiated, and therefore the ^{13}C–^{1}H couplings can be observed. As a consequence the signal of a methyl group will be a quadruplet, with a methylene being a triplet, etc. Because the coupling constants are very large, routinely more than 100 Hz, the spectrum can get very complex.

- A solution to this problem is **DEPT (Distortionless Enhancement by Polarization Transfer)** which is a technique which differentiates the different kinds of carbons through manipulation of the pulse sequences. In a DEPT spectrum, the phase of the signal will be different depending on the number of hydrogens attached to that particular carbon. Carbons with an odd number of hydrogens (1 or 3) will result in a positive peak, while carbons with an even number of hydrogens (2) give rise to a negative peak and the carbons without hydrogens show no peak.

- NMR can be obtained for atoms other than ^1H and ^{13}C. The most common other atoms are ^{19}F, ^{31}P, and ^{15}N.

- **Two-dimensional NMR techniques:** In these spectra there are two axes: each axis will be used by a spectrum and the two dimensional plot will show correlations between the atoms in the two spectra. In COSY, each axis has the representation of the same ^1H NMR spectrum. The diagonal of the 2-dimensional spectrum will represent all the signals in the spectra, but the off-diagonal signals will give information about the interactions between protons which are coupled to each other. The same effect can be obtained between a ^1H and ^{13}C spectrum; in this case it is known as HETCOR, and the off-diagonal peaks give information about which protons are coupled with which carbons. In NOESY (Nuclear Overhauser Effect), the off-diagonal peaks will indicate protons which are spatially close together.

- **MRI:** Magnetic Resonance Imaging is a very important diagnostic tool in modern medicine. A patient is placed in the large cavity of a large magnet and NMR spectra (proton) of cross-sections of the body are recorded. MRI picks up the signal of the hydrogens in the body, mostly from water molecules. Depending on the environment, these water molecules will result in different signals, and a three-dimensional image of the examined area can be obtained. Notice that the term "nuclear" is deleted in this medical application to avoid any misconceptions that these tests involve radioactive materials.

Ultraviolet Spectroscopy

The Basic Principles

A *conjugated system* can be described as consecutive π-orbitals found in a series of alternating double and single bonds. Examples of these types of systems are shown in Figure 2-42. Conjugated systems can be quite short, as in 1,3-butadiene and the allyl cation, or very long, as in β-carotene, which has eleven π-orbitals. Double bonds other than carbon-carbon double bonds can participate in conjugated systems, as shown by methyl vinyl ketone, where the carbon-oxygen double bond also participates in the multiple bonding. In order to be able to absorb UV light, a compound must have a conjugated system.

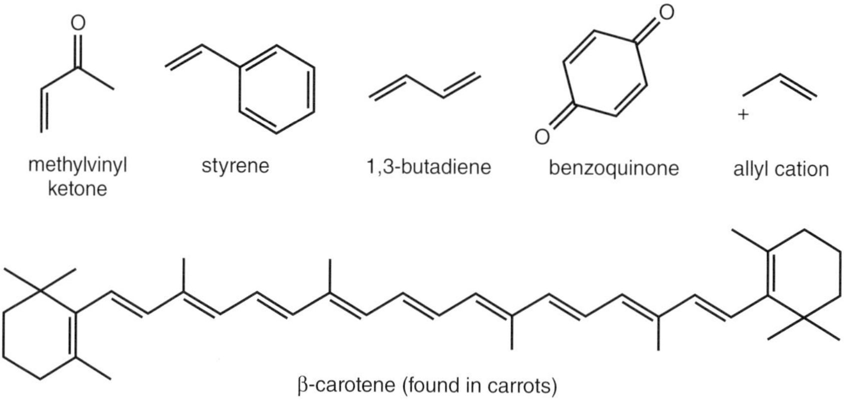

| methylvinyl ketone | styrene | 1,3-butadiene | benzoquinone | allyl cation |

β-carotene (found in carrots)

Figure 2-42. *Examples of conjugated systems.*

Molecular orbital theory (MO theory) accurately describes conjugated systems, the geometry of the orbitals involved, and their interactions with UV light. MO theory dictates that for every atomic orbital that participates in a bond, there is a corresponding number of *molecular orbitals*. To illustrate this, consider 1,3-butadiene, a simple conjugated system consisting of four sp^2 carbons. Each carbon has three hybrid orbitals in a trigonal planar arrangement, as well as an unhybridized p-orbital perpendicular to the plane of the hybridized orbitals. Since the four unhybridized p-orbitals participate in the conjugated system (as shown in Figure 2-43), four corresponding molecular orbitals are formed. Two of these orbitals, named ψ_1 and ψ_2, are bonding orbitals, which are the lowest in energy. The other two, ψ_3^* and ψ_4^*, are called *anti-bonding orbitals* (indicated by the asterisk), and are much higher in energy than the bonding orbitals. When electrons are found in the bonding orbitals, the bonding interaction between the two atoms at either end of the bond is strengthened. Likewise, when electrons are found in anti-bonding orbitals (a very high energy and unfavorable condition), the bonding interaction between the two orbitals on either end of the bond is weakened.

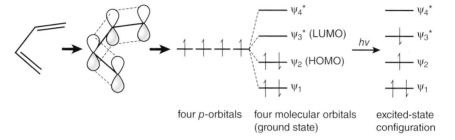

four p-orbitals   four molecular orbitals   excited-state
(ground state)   configuration

Figure 2-43. *Butadiene and corresponding molecular orbital diagram.*

Each of the four p-orbitals participating in the π-system has one electron, so the total number of electrons in the conjugated system in butadiene is four. These electrons are all found in the lowest energy orbitals, since this is the most stable configuration that promotes a bonding interaction between the carbons. This low energy configuration of electrons is called the *ground-state* configuration.

When one irradiates a conjugated system with UV light (commonly expressed as hν or sometimes simply "light"), the energy from the light is absorbed and an electron is promoted from the highest occupied molecular orbital ψ_2 (HOMO) to the lowest unoccupied molecular orbital ψ_3 (LUMO). This electronic transition, called a $\pi \rightarrow \pi^*$ transition, creates a new high energy configuration called the excited-state configuration, with a single electron in an antibonding orbital. As the system loses energy, the excited electron falls back down into ψ_2, and the ground-state configuration is restored.

The Instrument

A UV-Vis (ultraviolet-visible) spectrophotometer consists of a UV light source, in which the light beam is guided through a sample to a detector. The detector measures the intensity of the remaining light at the different wavelengths. The spectrum is generated by plotting the absorbance versus the wavelength, and shows the absorptions in the wavelength range from 200 to 800 nm (Figure 2-44).

The sample must be very dilute, normally in the 10^{-3} to 10^{-6} mol/L range. The solvent used cannot be UV-absorbing; common solvents are ethanol, chloroform, or dichloromethane.

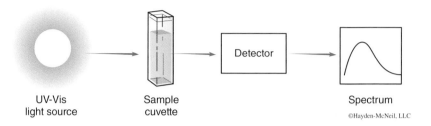

Figure 2-44. *Spectrophotometer.*

The sample is placed in a quartz cuvette, since glass absorbs in the UV range. A cuvette can be made of glass or plastic if the sample only absorbs in the visible light range. The standard path length of the light through the cuvette is 1 cm.

The classical setup of a UV-Vis spectrophotometer is an instrument on a bench, which contains the light and the detector. Optical fiber technology has greatly expanded the range of instrument assemblies, from submergible probes to detectors that fit on a computer card.

The Spectrum

A typical UV spectrum is acquired by plotting the absorbance of light by a sample as the wavelength of UV light is changed from 200 to 400 nm. The wavelengths of UV light required to effect the $\pi \rightarrow \pi^*$ transition are absorbed; this corresponds to the energy difference between the HOMO and the LUMO. For butadiene, the UV spectrum would appear as shown in Figure 2-45. Here, the maximum absorbance, called λ_{max}, occurs at 217 nm and the energy gap between the HOMO and LUMO can be calculated as follows:

$$E = \frac{hc}{\lambda} = \frac{(6.626 \times 10^{-34} \text{ Js}) \times (3.00 \times 10^8 \text{ ms}^{-1})}{2.17 \times 10^{-7} \text{ m}} = 9.16 \times 10^{-19} \text{ J}$$

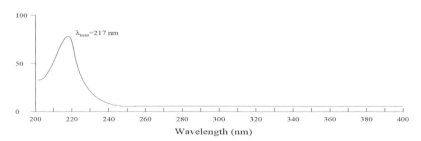

Figure 2-45. *UV spectrum of butadiene.*

The UV light is absorbed by a chromophore, the part of the molecule that is conjugated. The longer the chromophore, the higher the wavelength of maximum absorbance, λ_{max}. The λ_{max} is also dependent on the substitution on the conjugated system, but this is a smaller effect. Table 2-6 shows some typical λ_{max} values for conjugated systems. For molecules with long conjugated systems, such as carotene, the λ_{max} will shift to higher wavelength into the visible light region; these compounds are colored, indicating their absorption of visible light. The λ_{max} indicates that carotene absorbs at 451 nm, blue light, resulting in the observed orange color.

Table 2-6. Typical λ_{max} Values for Conjugated Systems

Compound	λ_{max} (nm)	Molar Absorptivity ε (L/mol cm)
1,3-butadiene	217	21,000
Isoprene (2-methyl-1,3-butadiene)	220	
1,3-cyclohexadiene	256	
Acrolein (2-propenal)	219	
1,3,5-hexatriene	258	35,000
1,3,5,7-octatetraene	290	
Carotene	451	139,500

Molar Absorptivity

The amount of UV light absorbed by a sample is directly proportional to the number of molecules in the path of the light. Lambert-Beer's law relates the percentage of light absorbed by a sample to its concentration and the *molar absorptivity* (ε, also called the *extinction coefficient*). The molar absorptivity is a physical constant unique to every conjugated compound. Lambert-Beer's law states that the absorbance (A) of light is directionally proportional to the concentration of the sample (c, mol/L), the path length traveled by the light (l, cm), and the molar absorptivity:

$$A = \varepsilon l c$$

Using this relationship with a known sample concentration, the molar absorptivity of the compound being studied can be calculated. In general, the molar absorptivities of most conjugated systems is between $\varepsilon = 10,000–25,000$.

Conversely, if the molar absorptivity of a compound is known, then the concentration of the sample can be determined using UV spectroscopy and Lambert-Beer's law.

Mass Spectrometry

The Basic Principles

Mass spectrometry analyzes molecules and particles according to mass. There are many variations of mass spectrometry instruments, but in its simplest setup, a sample is introduced in the gas phase and these molecules are bombarded by an electron beam, transforming them into charged particles. By applying a magnetic field, these charged particles are deflected according to their mass and focused on a detector.

When a molecule is ionized by an e-beam, a radical cation is formed; this is the molecular ion. Due to the inherent instability of charged particles, the molecular ion will fracture into smaller pieces, which can fracture into more fragment ions. The molecular ion and all the fragment ions are analyzed according to their mass/charge ratio, yielding structural information about the analyte (Figure 2-46).

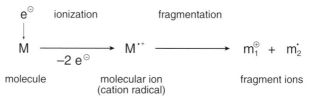

Figure 2-46. *Basic principle of mass spectrometry.*

The Instrument

A mass spectrometer has an injection port, an ionizer, an analyzer, and a detector (Figure 2-47).

Using a syringe, a sample is injected into a vacuum chamber at a temperature high enough to vaporize the sample; alternatively, a mass spectrometer (mass spec) can be connected to a gas chromatograph (GC/MS) or to an HPLC (LC/MS). In these combined instruments, the samples are analyzed as they elute from the column, and mass spectra are recorded for each fraction.

The sample is ionized by a high-energy electron beam (~70 eV). The electron beam strikes the molecules with enough energy to eject another electron from the molecule, resulting in a cation-radical. This process is called Electron Ionization or Electron Impact (EI). The original cation radical is the molecular ion $M^{+\cdot}$.

The charged particles are accelerated and deflected in a magnetic field. The molecular ion is unstable, so it will fragment into smaller ions called fragment ions. This fragmentation can occur at different sites in the molecule, leading to a collection of smaller fragment ions. Sometimes the molecular ion is so unstable that it cannot be detected.

Because the ions have different masses, they will be deflected at different angles by the magnetic field. This broad ion beam is focused on the detector, which records the m/z value (mass/charge ratio). The smaller the ion, the more they will be deflected. The detector gives a direct readout of the size of the ions and the intensity of the signal. In most cases the charge is equal to $1+$, $z = 1$.

More sophisticated mass spectrometers will have different injection methods, analyzers, and ionizers, depending on the particular properties of the sample. The result is always a spectrum giving the m/z ratio for the different fragments.

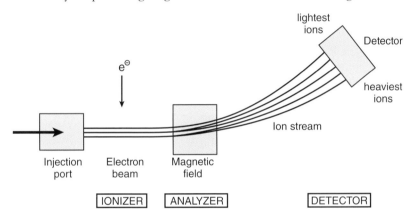

Figure 2-47. *Basic mass spectrometer.*

The Spectrum

A mass spectrum is a plot of the mass/charge (m/z) ratio versus relative abundance. As z is often equal to 1, the x-axis gives a direct readout of the mass of the molecular ion (if it can be detected) and the fragment ions. Calibration of the instrument is achieved by injecting a known compound and adjusting the instrument so that the weights are accurate.

The spectrum of *n*-octane is shown in Figure 2-48. Octane has a molecular weight of 114, and the molecular ion M^+ is seen in the spectrum.

The major fragment ions have m/z values of 85, 71, 57, 43, and 29. The peak at m/z 43 is the largest and is defined as the base peak; the base peak corresponds to the most abundant fragment ion and is assigned a relative abundance of 100 %. The relative abundance of all other peaks is measured in comparison to the base peak. A mass of 43 corresponds to a *n*-propyl cation.

The difference in m/z between the major peaks is indicated on the spectrum. A difference of 14 corresponds to the loss of a methylene CH_2, which is consistent with the linear structure of *n*-octane. The first major fragment lost has a mass of 29, corresponding to an ethyl group CH_3CH_2.

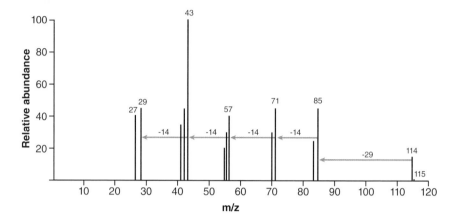

Figure 2-48. *Mass spectrum of* n-octane.

Starting from the *n*-octane molecule, the molecular ion M^+ splits off an ethyl group, yielding the fragment with an m/z value of 85: the *n*-hexyl cation. Consecutive losses of 14 explain the appearance of the other fragment ions, with the propyl cation being the ion with the highest abundance (Figure 2-49).

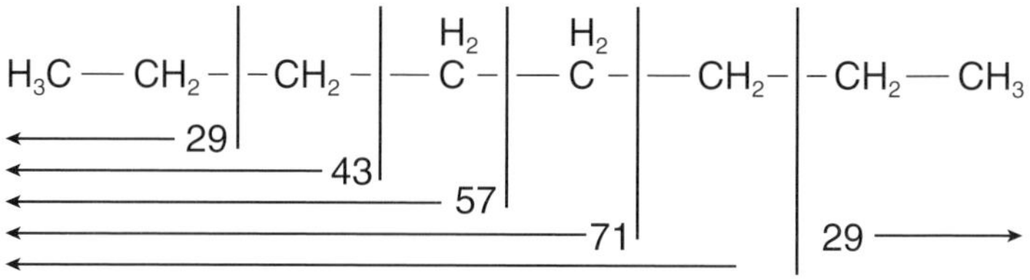

Figure 2-49. *Splitting pattern of* n-octane.

Isotope Patterns

Looking more closely at the mass spectrum of *n*-octane, a small peak at m/z 115 is noticed. This is an isotope peak and is due to the small percentage of ^{13}C present in the sample. If one of the eight carbons in *n*-octane is the ^{13}C isotope, the molecular weight of this molecular ion will be 115. The relative abundance of ^{13}C is 1.11 % compared to ^{12}C.

The intensity of the M + 1 peak in a compound with only C and H is equal to the intensity of the M peak × 1.11 % × # of C in the molecule. For *n*-octane in the spectrum in Figure 2-48, this would be equal to 15 × 1.11 % × 8 = 1.33 % relative abundance, which explains the small peak at 115.

Other elements have much more abundant isotopes than carbon and will display isotope peaks in the mass spectrum. The relative abundance of the most common isotopes in organic chemistry are listed in Table 2-7.

Table 2-7. Relative Abundance of Common Isotopes in Organic Molecules

Element	First Isotope	Second Isotope	Relative Abundance (%)
Carbon	^{12}C	^{13}C	1.11
Nitrogen	^{14}N	^{15}N	0.38
Sulfur	^{32}S	^{34}S	4.40
Chlorine	^{35}Cl	^{37}Cl	32.5
Bromine	^{79}Br	^{81}Br	98.0

For most molecules, the isotope peaks will be very small. But for compounds containing chlorine or bromine, the elements with the most abundant isotopes, very recognizable patterns of peaks will appear in the mass spectrum. For chlorine, the ratio of the molecular ion peak abundance and the peak at a mass two units higher, M/M + 2 is equal to 3/1. For bromine the M/M + 2 ratio is roughly 1/1, as the two isotopes are present in near-equal abundance.

The mass spectrum of 3-chloro-1-propene (Figure 2-50) shows the molecular ion peak at m/z 76, with the isotope peak at m/z 78, roughly about 1/3 the size. The base peak is at m/z 41, M − 35 (loss of chlorine), which corresponds to the allylic cation $CH_2=CH-CH_2^+$.

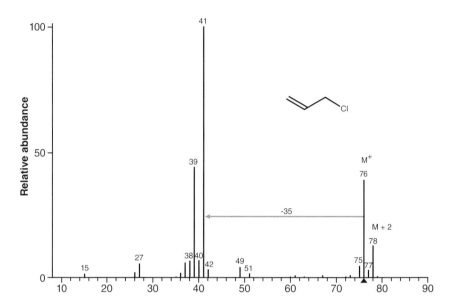

Figure 2-50. *Mass spectrum of 3-chloro-1-propene.*

The mass spectrum of bromobenzene in Figure 2-51 clearly shows the two peaks with almost equal abundance at m/z 156 (M) and m/z 158 (M + 2), as predicted by the natural abundance of the two isotopes of bromine, ^{79}Br and ^{81}Br. The base peak at m/z 77 corresponds to the phenyl cation.

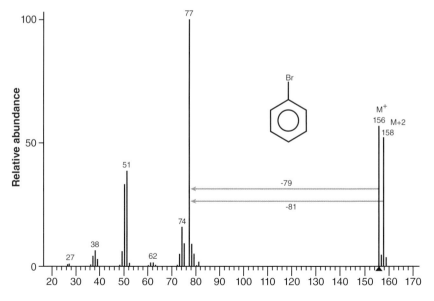

Figure 2-51. *Mass spectrum of bromobenzene.*

How to Interpret a Mass Spectrum

Mass spectra yield exact information about the mass of the ions that reach the detector; as organic molecules are constructed of similar building blocks, some fragment ions occur often. Conversely, the differences between peaks in the spectrum frequently correspond to specific molecules and molecular fragments. Table 2-8 lists some common fragment ions and frequent fragment losses.

Table 2-8. Common Fragment Ions and Common Fragments Losses in Mass Spectra

Fragment Ions	m/z	Fragments Lost	Mass Lost
Ethyl$^+$	29	H_2O	18
Propyl$^+$	43	OH	17
Butyl$^+$	57	CO	28
Methyl-CO$^+$	43	CO_2	44
Ethyl-CO$^+$	57	CH_3	15
Propyl-CO$^+$	71	CH_3CH_2	29
Phenyl$^+$	77	OCH_3	31
Benzyl$^+$ ($C_6H_5CH_2^+$)	91	$CH_2=CH_2$	28
Benzoyl$^+$ ($C_6H_5CO^+$)	105	CH_3CO	43

Some Representative Mass Spectra

Benzyl alcohol: The mass spectrum is shown in Figure 2-52. The molecular ion is clearly visible at m/z 108, along with its little isotope peak at 109. A very prominent peak is M − 1, loss of H, very common in alcohols. Loss of OH (−17) gives a peak at m/z 91, which is the benzylic cation—a rather stable cation—and very commonly seen in mass spectra. The base peak is m/z 79, which is protonated benzene. The phenyl cation is visible at m/z 77; the other peaks result from degradation of the benzene ring.

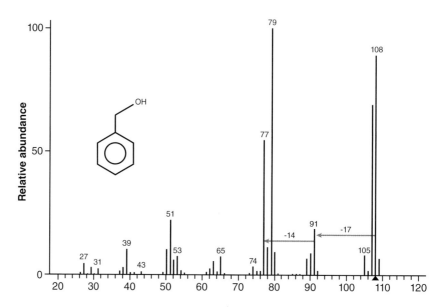

Figure 2-52. *Mass spectrum of benzyl alcohol.*

1-Hexanol: (Figure 2-53). In this mass spectrum the molecular ion at m/z 102 is not visible, indicating that it is not stable. The peak at m/z 84 corresponds to the loss of water (–18), very common for alcohols. The resulting hexene cation loses a methyl group (–15) to yield m/z 69. The base peak is at m/z 56, corresponding to $C_4H_8^+$, with the propyl cation at m/z 43 the next most abundant peak.

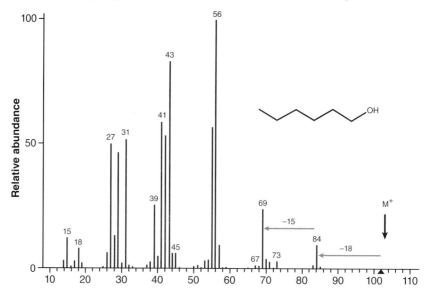

Figure 2-53. *Mass spectrum of 1-hexanol.*

Acetophenone: (Figure 2-54). The molecular ion M^+ is at m/z 120 (C_8H_8O). Loss of methyl (−15) yields the benzoyl cation, the base peak at m/z 105. Further loss of CO (−28) leads to the phenyl cation at m/z 77.

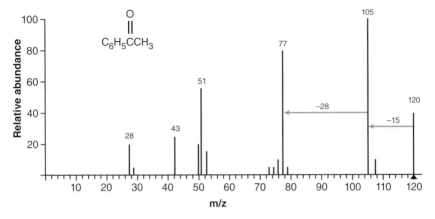

Figure 2-54. *Mass spectrum of acetophenone.*

Other Mass Spec Techniques

Many variations of the basic mass spectrometry technique have been developed over the years; now, different injection modes are possible as well as different ionizations and analyzers. The following list is not meant to be comprehensive, but will give some idea of the scope of the possibilities.

- **GC/MS:** A gas chromatograph (GC) is connected to a mass spectrometer (MS) inlet. An injected sample will be separated into its components by the GC, and the mass spec will detect the peaks as they elute off the column. The output of this experiment is a gas chromatogram with an accompanying mass spectrum for each peak.

- **LC/MS:** The sample is injected in an HPLC (high performance liquid chromatograph). The column will separate the different components of the sample, which are analyzed by the MS, analogous to the GC/MS method. In this case the instrument must be adapted to deal with the eluting solvent of the HPLC.

- **Different ionization systems:**
  - CI: Chemical Ionization instead of Electron Impact, which is a "softer" method to ionize the analytes.
  - ESI: Electrospray Ionization, which is often used for the analysis of proteins and other non-volatile samples. It is also a "softer" method, and ions are often carrying multiple charges using this ionization method.

- FAB: Ionization by Fast Atom Bombardment, which is also used for the analysis of peptides.
- MALDI: Matrix Assisted Laser Desorption Ionization, in which a matrix is mixed with the sample to accomplish ionization in a very "soft" way for sample with high masses.

• **Different analyzer systems:**

- Quadrupole Analyzer, which is an alternate method used to separate the charged fragments using four parallel metal rods.
- TOF: The Time of Flight method separates ions of different masses by using the differences in time to reach the detector.

Molecular Modeling

Molecules drawn on the page are two-dimensional representations of three-dimensional structures. This three-dimensional shape of a molecule is important because it governs the chemical and physical properties of the molecule.

Several kinds of software have been developed over the years to analyze molecular structures and to calculate properties of these structures. Thanks to molecular modeling the three-dimensional structure of a molecule can be visualized. In addition, information about the energy levels of the different shapes of the molecules can be calculated, and the most stable conformer can be determined. These methods are being used in different research areas, from predicting the feasibility of synthetic reactions to the forecasting the properties of new polymer molecules and the representation of very complex biochemical molecules.

Molecular graphics is used to display molecular structures. They can be as plain as simple line structures, and as complex and realistic as 3-D-type structures. These 3-D structures for example can show from which side a nucleophilic attack is feasible and which side is really hindered. Common programs like ChemDraw Ultra have the capability of showing the three-dimensional structure of molecules. Draw the molecule and convert to the 3-D model; double clicking on the 3-D model opens up a second window which allows you to rotate the molecule in different kinds of representations.

After a structure has been built and visualized, calculations can be performed to refine it to a stable and sterically logical conformation. *Molecular mechanics* is the technique that calculates the energy of a structure. By continuously varying the structure, molecular mechanics recalculates the energy at each interval and eventually delivers the conformation with the lowest energy; this is the optimum geometry. The result of minimization calculations usually yields a structure that is very close to the real structure. Molecular mechanics treats the molecule as a combination of charged masses coupled together with springs. Many different energy components are used in these calculations: bond stretching, torsion angles, hydrogen bonding, van der Waals attractions and repulsions, electrostatic attractions and repulsions, etc.

Molecular dynamics is the third facet of molecular modeling. Instead of looking at static models, molecular dynamics simulates the thermal motion of the most stable conformer of the molecule. Using the forces calculated using molecular mechanics, the possible motions of molecules can be visualized. The possible motions can also be compared to experimental data, like NMR data at different temperatures.

The most complete calculations use *quantum mechanics* to determine the energy of the different conformations; basically Schrodinger's equation is solved for the nuclei and electrons of the molecule. Several of these calculations methods are available as public domain programs; AMPAC and MOPAC are two representatives of these basic calculations.

Problems for Chapter 2

1. Find the structures and melting points for the following compounds.

   a. Biphenyl
   b. *p*-Cresol
   c. *trans*-Stilbene

2. If you had to measure the melting point of the compounds in Question 1 using the Mel-Temp apparatus, describe how you would use the higher and lower settings of the Mel-Temp to accurately measure these melting points.

3. If the determined melting points are 2–5 °C below the literature melting points, what does this mean?

4. Explain the difference in boiling points (you will have to look these up) between these different compounds with comparable molecular weights.

5. Look up and explain the boiling points in the following table.

Compound	MW	Boiling point	Compound	MW	Boiling point
(zigzag chain)			(ketone structure)		
(zigzag chain)			(ketone structure)		
(zigzag chain)			(ketone structure)		
(zigzag chain)			(ketone structure)		

6. Why is antifreeze (1,2-dihydroxyethane, bp 197 °C) added to the water in your radiator both in winter and summer?

7. Sodium chloride is added to water. What is the effect on the boiling point and on the melting point?

8. During one of the labs, Lucy G. has synthesized aspirin (acetylsalicylic acid), it does look nice and white, but the melting point is 70–74 °C. She is somewhat suspicious that maybe she did not get the correct compound. How could she prove that she actually did make aspirin? In the lab there is a hot plate, lots of thermometers, heating mantles, a Mel-Temp and lots of chemicals.

9. The observed optical rotation of a solution of R-limonene ($[\alpha]$ = +123°) in dichloromethane, measured at 20 °C, is 30.7°. The length of the sample cell is 10 cm. What is the concentration of limonene?

10. The measured refractive index of compound A, in a lab at room temperature of 27 °C, is 1.4605. Calculate the standard refractive index.

11. An unknown sample is being submitted for elemental analysis. The following results are obtained: 72.4 % C, 13.8 % H and 0 % N. Knowing that the sample's molecular weight is 116, what is the molecular formula of this compound? Propose a structure.

12. You have two samples: one is known to be acetophenone, while the other one is 1-phenylethanol. How would you know which one is which using infrared spectroscopy?

13. Luis A. reacted cyclohexene with H_2 in the presence of a Pd catalyst. How could Luis follow the reaction using IR?

14. Esterification of acetic acid with isopentanol in acidic conditions led to a liquid. Two carbonyl peaks are observed in IR: a large peak at 1730 cm^{-1}, with a smaller peak at 1715 cm^{-1}. Explain.

15. How would you decide which compound is which using only IR spectroscopy

    a. Benzoic acid and acetophenone
    b. Ethyl methyl ether and propanol
    c. Acetophenone and benzaldehyde
    d. 2-Cyanobutane and 2-methylbutanoic acid
    e. Phenol and cyclohexanol

16. Carolina Z. obtains a compound with molecular formula C_8H_8O, as shown by elemental analysis. The IR spectrum of her sample shows peaks at 3028, 1710 (strong), 1600 (sharp), and 1377 cm^{-1}.

17. Sketch the ^{1}H NMR spectrum of the following compounds:

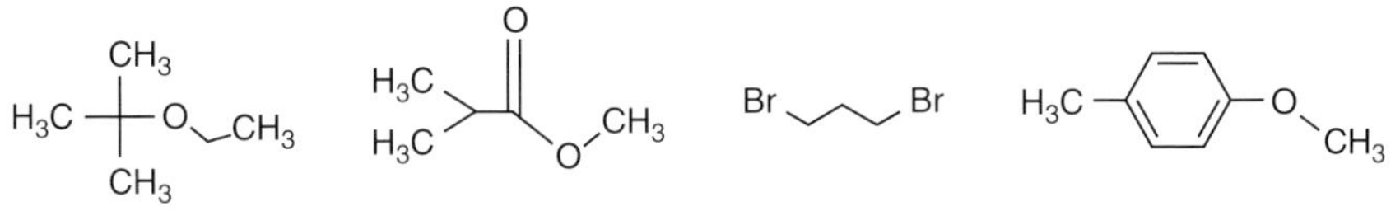

18. Sketch the ^{13}C NMR spectra of the compounds in Question 17.

19. Explain the peaks in the following mass spectra:

    a. 2-pentanone: m/e 86, 71, 57, 43 (100 %)
    b. 1,2-dichloroethane: m/e 100, 98, 64, 62 (100 %), 51, 49, 27
    c. Bromocyclohexane: m/e 163, 161 (both very small), 83 (100 %), 55, 41.

20. How would you decide which isomer is which using ^{1}H NMR spectroscopy?

    a. Diethyl ether and butanol
    b. Ethyl acetate and methyl propanoate
    c. Ethylbenzene and p-xylene (1,4-dimethylbenzene)
    d. 2-Hexene and 3-hexene

Purification Techniques

3

Recrystallization

What Is It Good For?

Let's begin with the question: how can a solid be purified? Hypothetically speaking, if the chunks of material were large enough to be seen and manipulated, the different crystals could be separated using pincers. For example, if cubic crystals of NaCl and flat crystals like naphthalene were mixed, it is possible to accomplish this separation. Of course, this would be quite a rough technique and not very practical; also, this feat could only be accomplished with large crystals. If the crystals are too small it becomes difficult, and it becomes totally impossible if the solids are powders.

In reality, a chemical reaction will very often result in an amorphous sludge, and a pure solid has to somehow be separated from this. In the area of natural products, on the other hand, chemists will start with large amounts of plant or animal material and from this material, an extremely small amount of a particular chemical must be isolated, such as taxol out of the bark of the yew tree.

For a mixture of solid compounds obtained in the lab, chemists often rely on the ability of these compounds to crystallize. To purify a solid compound, chemists use the differing solubilities of compounds in different solvents as well as the fact that the impurity will be present in a smaller amount than the desired product. The general technique involves dissolving the material to be crystallized in a hot solvent (or solvent mixture) and cooling the solution slowly. The solubility of a dissolved material decreases with decreasing temperatures; therefore, the solution will become oversaturated and the solid will separate from the solution as it is cooled. If the two compounds dissolved in the solvent have differing solubilities, it becomes possible to separate these two compounds. This process is called "Recrystallization" because it relies on dissolving crystals, which are then regenerated by crystallization.

The process to obtain purified sugar from either sugarcane or sugar beets is an excellent example of recrystallization. Several consecutive crystallization cycles lead to dark brown sugar, light brown sugar, and white sugar as the final products, each one more pure than the former fraction. The same principle is used to create those sugar sticks you receive with your coffee in fancy coffee shops: a wooden stick is placed in a saturated aqueous sugar solution and the crystals build up on the wooden stick; the longer you continue this process, the larger the crystals will be.

The Basic Principles

When using the recrystallization technique, the chemist relies on a basic principle of crystals: when crystals are being formed, the same individual molecules will fit in a specific crystal lattice structure. This phenomenon is called crystallization, an equilibrium process that produces very pure material.

Chemical compounds have different solubilities in different solvents, and this solubility is temperature dependent. Solubility curves have been determined for many compounds and can be found in the chemical literature. The solubility of a compound largely depends on the intermolecular interactions between the compound and the solvent, and on the polarity of both.

Sodium chloride is an ionic compound and is very polar; it is soluble in water at room temperature (300 g/L), and essentially insoluble in hexane no matter what the temperature. A non-polar compound like naphthalene is insoluble in water and has a nice solubility gradient in hexane; that is, it has low solubility at low temperature and high solubility at high temperature. On the other hand, a different pair of compounds could have rather similar solubilities in a particular solvent. For example, naphthalene and 2-methylnaphthalene behave very similarly because they have very similar structures.

If a concentrated hot solution is allowed to cool, crystals start to form (Figure 3-1). If the crystal formation is slow and nicely controlled, the crystal will only allow the same molecules to be incorporated in the crystal structure, excluding the molecules that don't fit in. It comes down to "segregation" on a molecular level and in this case, segregation is a good thing, because it leads to pure solids with the exclusion of impurities. A small seed crystal is formed initially, and it then grows layer by layer in a reversible manner.

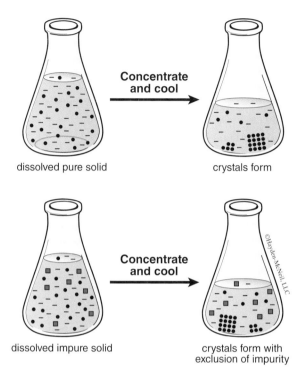

dissolved pure solid

Concentrate
and cool

crystals form

dissolved impure solid

Concentrate
and cool

©Hayden-McNeil, LLC

crystals form with
exclusion of impurity

Figure 3-1. *Crystallization.*

Recrystallization relies on the slow formation of crystals with the aim of obtaining pure materials. The impurity can be either more or less soluble than the compound you are interested in. If the impurity is not soluble at high temperature, it can be filtered off before the compound is crystallized. If the impurity is more soluble than the compound of interest, cooling the solution results in formation of pure crystals, with the impurity staying behind in the solution.

How Is It Done in the Lab?

Recrystallization can be done on many different scales, from kg or larger down to mg scale. The basic procedure is always the same, but the details will be somewhat different.

The first problem is to select a recrystallization solvent. Basic solvent properties were discussed in the "Solvents" section of Chapter 1. Ideally, the solvent should be a poor solvent at room temperature and a very good solvent at high temperature. To test this, place about 50 mg of the sample in a test tube. Add about 0.5 mL of a solvent at room temperature and stir the mixture by twirling the test tube. If most of the solid dissolves, your product is too soluble in this solvent. Repeat the procedure with a less polar solvent. If none or very few of the crystals dissolve at room temperature, heat the test tube in a hot water bath; if necessary, add more solvent to dissolve the crystals. If the crystals don't dissolve in refluxing solvent, repeat the procedure with a more polar solvent. If the crystals dissolved, allow the solution to cool to room temperature and then place it in an ice bath. If a lot of crystals develop, you have found a good solvent.

Picking a good solvent is something of an art. There is no perfect procedure, only trial and error accompanied by reasoning and common sense. You should feel free to mix solvents in any ratio to achieve the best recrystallization medium for your compound.

After a suitable solvent has been identified, the essential steps of a recrystallization are:

1. Dissolve the impure solid at high temperature.

2. Filter the solution if there is an insoluble fraction.

3. Cool the solution slowly to control the crystallization process.

4. Filter the formed crystals.

5. Dry the crystals.

On a large scale:

1. Use an Erlenmeyer flask to mix the solid with the solvent. The Erlenmeyer flask is slightly preferable to a beaker because its conical shape minimizes evaporation of the solvent.

2. Use a hot plate to heat the solution and a stir bar or boiling chips to prevent excessive bumping.

3. If part of the solid does not dissolve, the solution should be filtered hot to remove these insolubles. Hot filtration can be accomplished by heating the filter, by using hot solvent first, or by heating the funnel in a heating mantle with a hole on the bottom. The solution is collected in a second, heated Erlenmeyer flask.

4. To cool the solution, turn off the hot plate, but leave the solution on the heated surface to avoid rapid cooling.

5. After crystals have formed, the yield can be increased by cooling the Erlenmeyer flask in an ice bath.

6. Filter the solution using either gravity filtration or a Büchner funnel with a suction flask connected to vacuum.

7. "Wash" the crystals with a minimal amount of cold solvent to remove any impurities that might have adhered to the surface of the crystals.

8. Dry either in air, by leaving the crystals on top of the filter and continuing to pull vacuum, or by placing the crystals in a drying tube or desiccator.

9. Weigh the product.

10. Check the purity by measuring the melting point and/or running some spectra.

11. Repeat if necessary.

On a small scale:
The basic steps are the same as in the recrystallization on a large scale, but depending on the amount of material, different glassware should be used.

- For smaller recrystallization, a smaller-size Erlenmeyer flask or a test tube should be used. Different sizes of filtration flasks and filters are available, and the appropriate size should always be used.

- For 10–100 mg microscale, Craig tubes are sometimes used. As shown in Figure 3-2, a Craig tube looks like a test tube, with a narrowing on top. A slightly rough glass piece fits into the opening on top. To recrystallize a compound, the solution is placed in the Craig tube and concentrated, if necessary. Upon cooling, the glass "stopper" piece is inserted in the top of the tube and the crystals form on the bottom of the tube. The Craig tube is then inverted in a centrifuge tube and the whole assembly is placed in a centrifuge, with an equal weight on the opposite side. Centrifugation will force the solvent out of the Craig tube into the centrifuge tube, while the crystals will remain in the Craig tube.

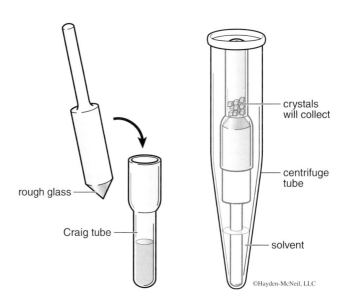

Figure 3-2. *Craig tube.*

Different recrystallization scenarios:

Purification by recrystallization can be successful when there is a large difference in solubility between the compound of interest and the impurity. However, it will also work when the solubility is almost identical, assuming the impurity is present in a smaller quantity.

• If there is a large difference in the solubility of the material to be crystallized in hot and cold solvent, the solubility-temperature curve is steep.

The detailed calculation of every step in the following recrystallization may help you to better understand what is really going on during the dissolving, heating and cooling processes (Figure 3-3). Assume you are performing a recrystallization on substance A contaminated with impurity B. You already picked a solvent for the recrystallization: the solubilities of A at 20 °C is 1 mg/mL and at 100 °C, 100 mg/mL; the solubilities for B at 20 °C is 50 mg/mL and at 100 °C, 100 mg/mL.

Some impurity B might dissolve at low temperature, but most B is trapped in the A crystals. Upon heating to 100 °C, all of A and B dissolve. If the cooling is nicely controlled, the B impurity will stay in solution and only A will crystallize. The A crystals can then be filtered off and dried.

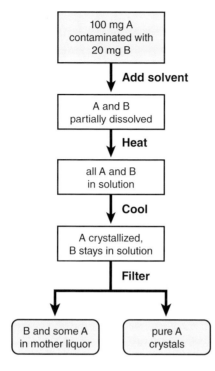

Figure 3-3. *Recrystallization flow chart.*

- A material can also be purified by recrystallization when both the desired substance and the impurity have similar solubilities, as long as the impurity represents a small fraction of the total solid. This scenario is shown in Figure 3-4. Assume again you are performing a recrystallization on substance A contaminated with impurity B, but in this case the solubilities of A and B are identical: at 20 °C the solubility is 10 mg/mL and at 100 °C, the solubility is 100 mg/mL for both A and B. In this case the end result is not quite as intuitive, but if B is present as an impurity, repeated cycles of dissolving and crystallization will still lead to pure product A, as shown in the graphic presentation in Figure 3-4.

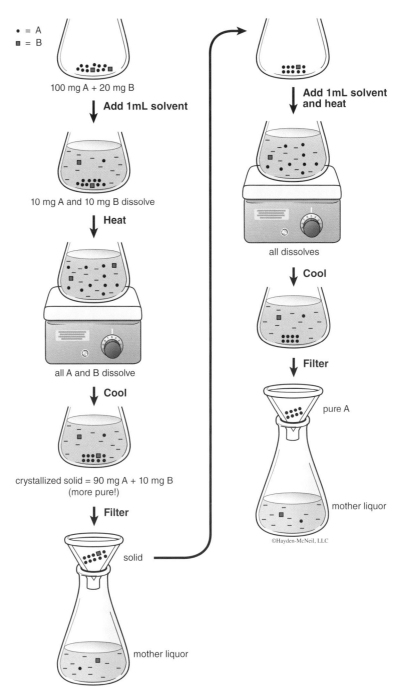

Figure 3-4. *Purification by recrystallization.*

Small amounts of A and B dissolve at room temperature, but all material dissolves when the solution is heated. Upon cooling, crystals of A will form, but A will still be contaminated with B, but there will be less B than before. In this case, another cycle of dissolving and crystallization will lead to pure A.

Practical Tips

- Patience will be rewarded in recrystallization. The slower a solution is allowed to cool, the purer the crystals will be. A good trick is to turn off the hot plate and leave the Erlenmeyer flask on top of the hot plate as it slowly cools down.

- If a solution gets oversaturated and crystals do not start to form spontaneously, a few tricks can be used: either toss in a very small crystal of the material to "seed" the solution, or scratch the surface of the flask with a spatula. The hard steel of the spatula will slightly etch the glass, which creates a sharp edge giving the crystals a place to start growing. If the solvent is miscible with water, as ethanol is, you can try putting in a very small ice crystal: this will reduce the solubility of the solute in the immediate vicinity of the ice, and provide a sharp edge for crystal growth.

- Cooling the solution in an ice bath or leaving it in the refrigerator or freezer overnight can lead to good yields of recovery.

- The mother liquor, which is the solution you obtain after filtration, will still contain some of your compound. Concentrate the solution and cool it again, which will yield you a second crop. Often this crop is not as pure as the first crop and may have to be recrystallized again.

- Colored impurity can be removed by heating the solution with activated charcoal, which of course turns the solution pitch black. After refluxing for a few minutes, the hot solution must be filtered to remove the charcoal, then pure compound can be crystallized out.

- An oil can form rather than a solid; this often happens if a compound whose melting point is lower than the solvent's boiling point is recrystallized. If this oil solidifies, it will contain many impurities. Different solvents could be added to prevent the oil formation, or you can try to seed crystal formation before the oil starts to form.

- Mixed solvents can be used for recrystallization. Ethanol or methanol/water mixtures are often used, or a polar organic solvent such as chloroform or dichloromethane can be mixed with the much less polar hexanes. Sometimes the solid can be dissolved in one solvent; another solvent is then added until the mixture just turns cloudy. The mixture is then allowed to cool very slowly.

Extraction

What Is It Good For?

Mixtures of compounds can be separated in many fashions. Many methods rely on partition processes; that is, the compounds in question show more affinity for one environment than for another. In the chromatographic processes, which will be discussed below, the partition is between stationary and mobile phases. The partition can also be between two liquid phases (two different solvents), or between a solid and a liquid phase; these are both called extraction. If the two solvents are immiscible, any dissolved compound will have more affinity for one solvent over another, and extraction will rely on this principle to separate different compounds. On the other hand, a solid-liquid extraction pulls one or more compounds out of the solid mixture into a solvent.

Let's look at Italian dressing as an example of liquid-liquid extraction. Italian dressing has two major components, vinegar and oil (Figure 3-5). The vinegar is the aqueous phase, which contains about 5 % acetic acid. The oil layer is an organic phase and is immiscible with the aqueous layer. If salt is added to the vinegar/oil mixture, it will dissolve in the aqueous phase because it is water-soluble and insoluble in the organic phase (oil). If we add an herb to the dressing, such as thyme, the essence of the thyme (the organic compounds that give thyme its particular taste) is soluble in the organic phase—the oil. The salt and essence of thyme are partitioned between the two immiscible layers, all contributing to the taste of the Italian dressing.

©Hayden-McNeil, LLC

Figure 3-5. *Italian dressing.*

The same principles can be applied in the lab. A mixture of two compounds, one water-soluble and one water-insoluble, can be separated by adding both water and an organic solvent. The water-soluble component is soluble in the water phase, the other component is soluble in the organic solvent. If the organic solvent and the water are immiscible the two layers can be separated, thereby accomplishing the separation of the two compounds in question. This is the simplest example of a liquid-liquid extraction, which relies on the different solubilities of compounds in different immiscible solvents.

Making coffee is an example of a solid-liquid extraction. The coffee beans are ground to increase their surface area, then placed in a filter. Boiling water is poured over the grounds, thereby "extracting" the active ingredients of coffee in the aqueous phase. The less water you use and the longer you extract the coffee grounds, the more concentrated the coffee solution will be.

A similar process can be done in the lab to extract active ingredients out of natural products, such as plant or animal material. In this case, organic solvents, rather than water, will typically be chosen. Chemists have designed rather sophisticated setups to accomplish these difficult extractions of sometimes minute amounts of active ingredients.

The Basic Principles

Liquid-Liquid Extraction

Liquid-liquid extraction is based on the varying solubilities of different solutes in immiscible solvents. The two solvents will form two layers; the solvent with the lowest density will be the top layer. The densities of common solvents are included in Chapter 1, Table 1-2. The organic solvent will almost always be lighter than the aqueous layer, except for the chlorinated solvents. A separatory funnel is commonly used, as shown in Figure 3-6.

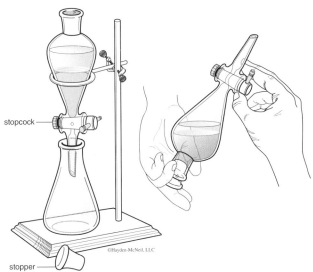

stopcock

stopper

©Hayden-McNeil, LLC

Figure 3-6. *Liquid–liquid extraction.*

Let's assume we have a mixture of acetaminophen and sodium chloride. Acetaminophen, the active ingredient in Tylenol, is soluble in ethyl acetate ($CH_3COOCH_2CH_3$) and very slightly soluble in cold water, while sodium chloride is very soluble in water but insoluble in ethyl acetate. If both ethyl acetate and water are added, the acetaminophen will be in the ethyl acetate layer and the salt in the water phase, and the two can be separated.

If a mixture of two compounds is dissolved in a solvent, the addition of a second immiscible solvent results in the formation of a second layer. Now the molecules (the solute) have a choice: solvent I or solvent II. The ratio of concentrations of a solute in each layer is defined by the partition coefficient K, the distribution constant.

$$K = C_2/C_1$$

where C_2 is the concentration of the solute in solvent 2 and C_1 is the concentration of this same solute in solvent 1 in g/L. The partition coefficient is a constant for each solute that is dependent on the pair of solvents used.

Assume an organic compound **A** has a partition coefficient between water and ethyl acetate equal to 8, and 10 g of **A** is dissolved in 100 mL of water. If 20 mL of ethyl acetate are added, you can calculate how much **A** remains in the water layer (x g) using this equation:

$$K = 8 = \frac{\dfrac{10\ g - x\ g}{20\ mL}}{\dfrac{x\ g}{100\ mL}}, \text{ solving for } x \text{ leads to } x = 3.8\ g$$

This means that of the original 10 g **A**, 6.2 g are in the ethyl acetate layer and 3.8 g are in the aqueous layer. The ethyl acetate layer is separated.

A second extraction of the aqueous layer with another 20 mL of ethyl acetate leads to the following equation:

$$K = 8 = \frac{\dfrac{3.8\ g - y\ g}{20\ mL}}{\dfrac{y\ g}{100\ mL}}, \text{ solving for } y \text{ leads to } y = 1.5\ g$$

The second extraction results in 2.3 g of **A** in the organic layer. Combining both ethyl acetate layers yields 8.5 g **A**, and a higher recovery can be obtained by continuing the extractions, or by using more ethyl acetate in each extraction.

Acid-Base Extraction

Acid-base extraction is a very powerful method for purifying mixtures in the work-up procedure of a reaction. Organic acids and bases in their neutral form are soluble in organic solvents, but the corresponding salts are water-soluble. Converting acids and bases to the corresponding salt gives us a convenient tool to separate acidic, alkaline and neutral organic compounds. Acid-base extractions are the same as liquid-liquid extractions as far as manipulation of glassware is concerned.

The principles of acid-base extractions are illustrated in Figure 3-7 and 3-8. A mixture of an acidic compound **A**, a basic compound **B**, and a neutral compound **N** can be separated into its components using the following extraction scheme:

- Carboxylic acids are, as a general rule, soluble in diethyl ether. Addition of aqueous sodium hydroxide to the mixture of **A**, **B**, and **N**, dissolved in an organic solvent, will convert the acid to the corresponding sodium carboxylate. **B** and **N** will not react, and they will stay in the organic layer. The salt of the carboxylic acid is now water-soluble. Separation of the organic and aqueous layers is followed by reacidification of the aqueous layer with an acid such as hydrogen chloride; this will reconstitute the carboxylic acid in its original form. Because the acidic compound **A** is once again organic-soluble, it can be extracted with an organic solvent. The acid **A** is now isolated from the mixture.

- The converse can be done with alkaline organics such as amines. Addition of aqueous hydrogen chloride to the organic layer converts the basic amine **B** to the ammonium chloride salt, which makes it water-soluble. The organic and aqueous layers are separated, with the organic layer now only containing the neutral component **N**. Evaporation of the organic solvent yields isolated **N**.

- The base **B** is still in the aqueous layer as the ammonium salt. Addition of aqueous sodium hydroxide frees the base converting it back to **B** and it becomes once again organic-soluble. Extraction with the organic solvent, followed by evaporation, recovers the basic component of the mixture **B**.

How Is It Done in the Lab?

Extractions can be done on several scales. On a large scale (larger than 50 mL total), separatory funnels (sep funnels) are used. As shown in Figure 3-6, they are conical-shaped and have a stopcock at the bottom to accurately control the release of liquid. A ring stand is used to hold the sep funnel in place.

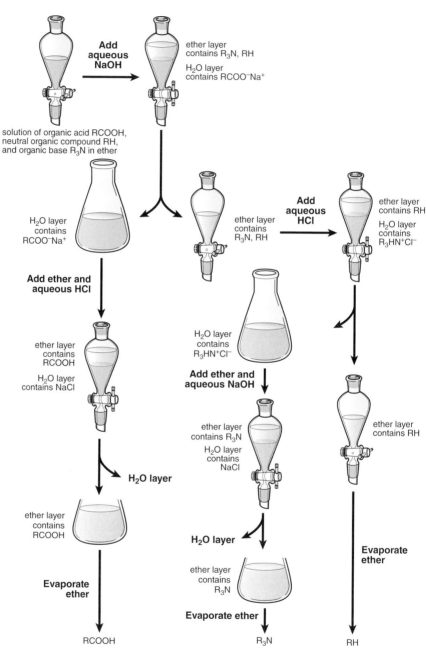

Figure 3-7. *Acid–base extraction.*

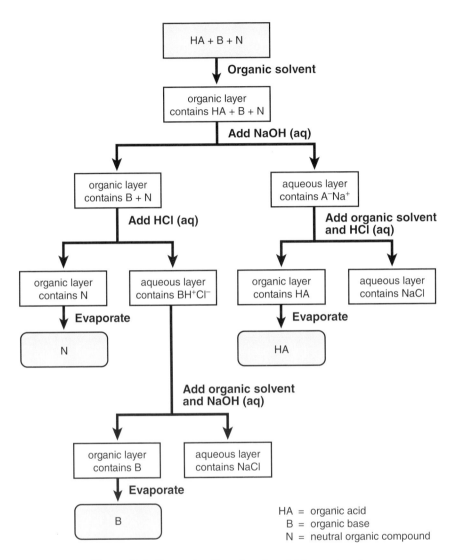

Figure 3-8. *Extraction flow chart in acid–base extraction.*

The following steps describe an extraction procedure *on a large scale*:

1. Choose a separatory funnel that is at least twice the volume of all liquids involved.

2. Place the sep funnel in the ring stand and, with a funnel, add the solution to be extracted and the other solvent.

3. Close the sep funnel with the stopper. Make sure there is a tight fit; use a small amount of grease if necessary. Be aware that the organic solvent might dissolve the grease, which would contaminate your compound.

4. Grab the sep funnel with both hands, one hand holding the top part with a finger on the stopper and the other hand controlling the stopcock.

5. Immediately invert the funnel and open the stopcock to release the pressure. Repeated venting will be necessary during the extraction, otherwise the pressure build-up inside the funnel might push the stopper out and you would lose all your compound. The pressure can be due to low boiling solvents, such as ether, or to formation of CO_2 in acid-base extractions.

6. Gently shake the funnel to assure maximum contact between the two layers. Don't shake too much or you might form an emulsion, which will take a very long time to separate.

7. Replace the funnel in the ring stand and immediately remove the stopper. If you don't, the stopper may get stuck due to some negative pressure inside the sep funnel.

8. Once the layers are nicely separated, drain off the bottom layer in an Erlenmeyer flask. When most of the bottom layer is drained, you may have to swirl the funnel around a bit to get as much separation between the two layers as possible.

9. Pour off the top layer through the top of the funnel.

10. Repeat the extraction if necessary.

11. Combine the organic layers.

12. Dry the organic layer before proceeding (see below).

13. Evaporate the solvent (described in the Distillation section).

14. NEVER discard a fraction until you are absolutely sure that you have your compound.

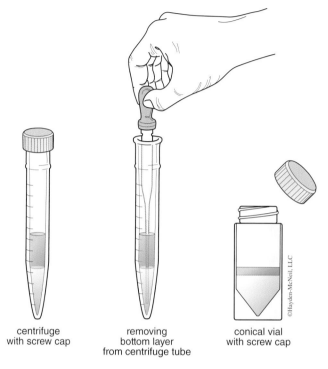

with screw cap

removing
bottom layer
from centrifuge tube

conical vial
with screw cap

©Hayden-McNeil, LLC

Figure 3-9. *Liquid–liquid extraction on microscale.*

The extraction procedure on a *microscale*, as illustrated in Figure 3-9, is essentially the same as in macroscale extractions:

1. If working with less than 500 mg, a sep funnel becomes impractical; in this case, centrifuge tubes or conical vials and Pasteur pipets are used for extractions. The conical shape of these containers allows you to perform very accurate separations on a small scale.

2. Place the solution to be extracted in the vial, then add the organic solvent. Stopper the container and very gently shake. Make sure you vent the container very carefully and frequently.

3. Centrifuge if the layers don't separate cleanly.

4. Remove the bottom layer and transfer.

5. Repeat the extraction a second time.

6. Combine the organic layers, dry and evaporate the solvent.

Practical Tips

- Always place the centrifuge tube or the vial in a beaker; it helps to stabilize it and can catch spills.

- Centrifuge tubes can handle up to 15 mL, while the conical vials are also practical for smaller amounts of solvent.

- Transferring the liquids is done using a Pasteur pipet with a bulb, which takes some practice. A few tips:

  - When transferring solutions from one vial to another, hold both vials in one hand, side by side, to minimize the distance your hand has to travel with the full Pasteur pipet.
  - To remove the bottom layer, expel the air from the bulb before inserting the pipet in the liquid, then slowly draw the lower layer into the pipet. Immediately drain the liquid into another vial.
  - If necessary, you can also remove the top layer with a pipet, though it is not easy to do this as efficiently as removing the bottom layer.

- The relative densities of the two solvents used are extremely important because the densities will determine which will be the top layer. For most organic solvents the top layer is the organic layer, but halogenated solvents have a higher density than water and will be on the bottom.

- Never assume that you are absolutely sure which one is the top layer, because the density can be affected by the compounds dissolved in the solvents. Therefore, never discard any layers until you are absolutely sure that you have isolated your compound.

- Always label all fractions. If you lose track and are not sure which flask contains the aqueous layer, pipet a small amount in a test tube and add some water. If it remains one layer, it was the aqueous phase.

- Remember to vent often. Pressure will build up in the sep funnel when shaken.

- Don't forget to remove the stopper as soon as you place the funnel in the ring stand; otherwise, it might get stuck.

- Always place a container under a sep funnel hanging in a ring stand. Stopcocks have been known to leak!

- More efficient extractions can be accomplished by "salting out." Addition of salt crystals, brine (a saturated NaCl solution), or sodium sulfate make the aqueous layer more polar, which will decrease the solubility of an organic compound in the aqueous layer. This results in better and more effective extraction of the organic compound in the organic layer.

- An emulsion can form and prevent the layers from separating cleanly. Either the whole content of the sep funnel is an emulsion or, more often, a third layer will form between the organic and aqueous layer. In this case,

    - Wait for several minutes and see if the layers will separate spontaneously.
    - Gently swirl the liquids in the sep funnel.
    - You can also drain the separated aqueous layer, then add more water to break the emulsion.
    - If all else fails, you can filter the content of the sep funnel through Celite to break the emulsion, then return the filtrate to the sep funnel.
    - In microscale extractions, centrifuging will separate the layers. Centrifugation is also an option for macroscale, but you need a large-scale centrifuge.
    - The salting out method described above can also break the emulsion; try adding some brine to the sep funnel.

- After an acid or base extraction of the organic layer, the organic layer is always washed at least once with pure water to remove any remaining inorganic acid or base.

- If the organic layer is the bottom layer, it is good practice to drain the organic layer (macroscale or microscale), add more organic solvent to perform the second extraction, combine both organic layers, and rinse the sep funnel before washing the organic layers.

Drying the Organic Fractions

The end result of an extraction is a solution in an organic solvent that has been in contact with an aqueous layer. Because water has some solubility in organic solvents, this solution will contain some water, which must be removed to proceed. The solution has to be *dried;* that is, the water must be removed.

These solutions are dried using chemical drying agents; the commonly used drying agents are anhydrous inorganic salts, which can accept water into their crystal structure to form hydrates.

$$MgSO_4 \text{ (anhydrous)} + H_2O \rightleftharpoons MgSO_4 \cdot xH_2O$$

$$x = 1\text{--}7$$

Drying agents are ranked according to their rate of water absorption, their capacity (how much water can they absorb), their effectiveness (level of dryness achieved) and their chemical nature (acidic or alkaline) and inertness. Polar solvents such as ether and ethyl acetate retain quite a bit of water, and therefore need drying agents with high drying capacity. Rather non-polar solvents such as petroleum ether and chloroform do not retain much water and are easier to dry. Drying agents are available in powder and/or granular form, and this also has an effect on their use. Table 3-1 gives information about drying agents.

How Is It Done in the Lab?

- Dry the solution, not the neat compound. If the compound you wish to dry is not dissolved, add some solvent before drying. Drying neat compounds results in too much loss, because some compound will adhere to the drying agent.

  How much drying agent should you add? First, add a small amount of drying agent and wait for it to clump together. Keep adding drying agent until some granules float freely in the solution.

- After adding drying agent to the solution, swirl the solution to increase the contact between the solution and the drying agent and thus accelerating the drying process. A magnetic stirrer could be used for this process.

- A drying time of ~10 minutes is optimal. Stopper the container if necessary.

- The drying agent should be removed. Filtration is the preferred method: either gravity filtration using filter paper or vacuum filtration using a Büchner or Hirsch funnel. For microscale experiments, a Pasteur pipet can be used to remove the solution from the drying agent; a Pasteur filter pipet or a pipet with a cotton plug can be used for increased efficacy (Figure 3-10). In the case of a granular drying agent, decantation is sometimes a possibility.

- When using a drying agent in powder form, wash the drying agent with solvent after filtration, as too much material can stick to the drying agent and reduce the yield. With a granular drying agent, it is also good practice to wash the drying agent.

- As illustrated in Figure 3-10, a Pasteur pipet filled halfway with drying agent can be used as a drying tube. This should only be used with highly efficient, fast-drying agents, such as $CaSO_4$.

- Solid products can be dried in a vacuum oven or in a desiccator containing drying agent: the solid product is placed in a small beaker, Petri dish or watch glass, the desiccant can be separated from the latter container with a mesh screen or porcelain plate. Alternatively, a homemade desiccator, such as a large screw top jar, can be used. The drying process is accelerated if a vacuum is applied to the desiccator (Figure 3-11).

Table 3-1. Properties of Common Drying Agents

Drying Agent	Acid-base Behavior	Capacity	Effective-ness	Comments
$MgSO_4$	Neutral	High	Medium	Good multipurpose drying agent; exists in powder and granular form; has the ability to absorb a lot of water.
$CaSO_4$ (Drierite)	Neutral	Low	High	Very fast and efficient drying agent, but a lot of drying agent might be necessary. Drierite often contains a blue indicator, which turns pink when hydrated. Often used in desiccators.
Na_2SO_4	Neutral	High	Low	Only good for pre-drying.
$CaCl_2$	Neutral	Medium	Medium	Often used in drying tubes.
KOH	Alkaline	High	High	Very effective for basic compounds, such as amines. Caustic.
K_2CO_3	Alkaline	Low	Medium	Only for alkaline compounds.
H_2SO_4	Acidic	High	High	Used in desiccators, cannot be used to dry solutions directly. Indirect drying is an option.

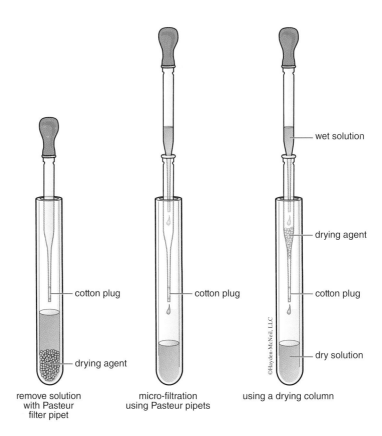

cotton plug

cotton plug

wet solution

drying agent

cotton plug

drying agent

dry solution

remove solution
with Pasteur
filter pipet

micro-filtration
using Pasteur pipets

using a drying column

©Hayden-McNeil, LLC

Figure 3-10. *Different methods for removing drying agent in microscale.*

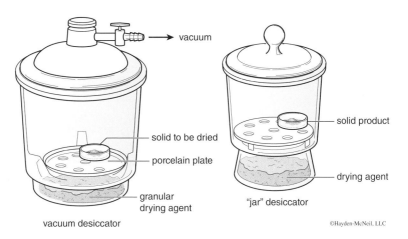

vacuum

solid to be dried

porcelain plate

granular
drying agent

vacuum desiccator

solid product

drying agent

"jar" desiccator

©Hayden-McNeil, LLC

Figure 3-11. *Desiccator.*

Distillation

What Is It Good For?

Distillation is the process of vaporizing a liquid, condensing the vapor, and collecting the condensate in another container. This technique is very useful for separating a liquid mixture when the components have different boiling points, or when one of the components will not distill.

An example of distillation is an alcohol "still" known to almost all cultures in the world. Fermentation of grains or fruits, such as grapes, leads to alcohol formation and eventually either beer or wine. The amount of alcohol produced by fermentation is limited to ~12 %, because the higher alcohol content kills the alcohol-producing enzymes. To obtain stronger liquors with higher alcohol content, distillation is necessary, and there is evidence that very early human civilizations knew how to distill alcohol. In distillation, the liquid mixture is heated and the lower boiling fraction, in this case ethyl alcohol, will evaporate; it is then condensed and collected in a receptacle. Distillation can produce liquors of up to 95 % ethyl alcohol.

Distillation is one of the principal methods of purifying a liquid in the laboratory. Four basic distillation methods are available to the chemist: simple distillation, fractional distillation, vacuum distillation (distillation at reduced pressure), and azeotropic distillation.

On a Molecular Level

The boiling point corresponds to the temperature at which the vapor pressure of a compound equals the external pressure exerted on a liquid. Therefore, a liquid boils when molecules are able to escape the surface of the liquid.

On a molecular level, as the liquid is heated, more energy is added to the liquid phase. At some point, the molecules of the lowest boiling component will have enough energy to escape from the liquid phase into the gas phase (Figure 3-12). Equilibrium will establish itself, with molecules evaporating, while other molecules in the gas phase will recondense into the liquid phase as they lose their energy. As the liquid continues to be heated, more energy is introduced in the system and more molecules will evaporate, filling the distillation apparatus and reaching the condenser. The liquid phase will be at a constant temperature as long as there are molecules with the same boiling point, because the additional heat (energy) added into the system is used by the molecules to evaporate. The gas phase also displays the same temperature.

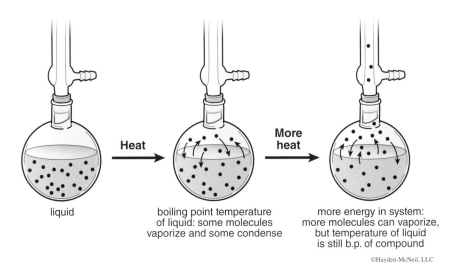

liquid

boiling point temperature
of liquid: some molecules
vaporize and some condense

more energy in system:
more molecules can vaporize,
but temperature of liquid
is still b.p. of compound

©Hayden-McNeil, LLC

Figure 3-12. *Boiling point.*

Distillation at atmospheric pressure is not always possible; for example, for rather large molecules the boiling point becomes unreachable at atmospheric pressure. The compound would decompose at the high temperatures necessary to vaporize it. However, because the boiling point is dependent on the pressure (see the section on Boiling Points in Chapter 2), the distillation at reduced pressure, under vacuum, becomes possible.

Simple Distillation

A simple distillation is used to purify a compound that is almost pure already (less than 10 % impurity), or if the impurities are non-volatile. A real-life example would be the distillation of seawater. When distilled, seawater results in potable water, and the residue consists of all the different salts that had been present in the seawater. This method is always an option considered when the desalination of seawater is discussed, but the energy needed to accomplish this simple process is exorbitant and would result in very expensive water. Alternative heating methods, such as the use of solar energy, make this process feasible in certain circumstances.

In simple distillation, vapor rises from the distillation flask and comes into contact with a thermometer that records its temperature (Figure 3-13). The vapor passes through a condenser, which re-liquefies the vapor and guides it into the receiving flask. The temperature observed during the distillation of a pure substance remains constant throughout the distillation, as long as both vapor and liquid are present in the system.

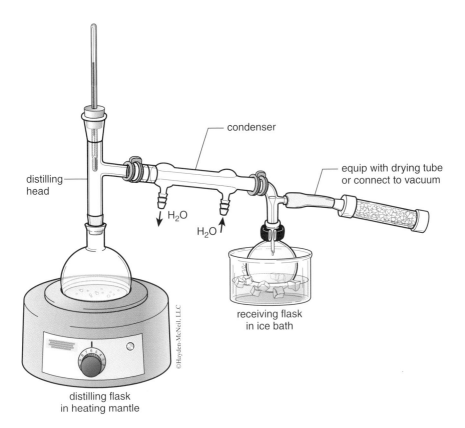

condenser

equip with drying tube
or connect to vacuum

distilling
head

H_2O

H_2O

receiving flask
in ice bath

©Hayden-McNeil, LLC

distilling flask
in heating mantle

Figure 3-13. *Simple distillation setup.*

When a liquid mixture is distilled, often the temperature does not remain constant but increases throughout the distillation. If the two components are miscible, such as benzene and toluene, the vapor pressure above the liquid will be the sum of the two individual vapor pressures (Raoult's law). The partial vapor pressure for each component will depend on the vapor pressure of the pure component and the mole fraction of that component. A mole fraction is the ratio of the moles of one component to the total number of moles present in the system:

N_B = mole fraction of benzene = moles benzene/(moles of benzene + moles toluene)

N_T = mole fraction of toluene = moles toluene/(moles of benzene + moles toluene)

The partial pressure of benzene equals

$$P_B = N_B \times P_B^\circ$$

in which P_B° represents the vapor pressure of pure benzene.

The same equation is valid for toluene

$$P_T = N_T \times P_T^\circ$$

in which P_T° represents the vapor pressure of pure toluene.

If Dalton's law of partial pressures is applied, the total vapor pressure of the solution can be calculated as the sum of the two partial pressures:

$$P_{solution} = P_T + P_B$$

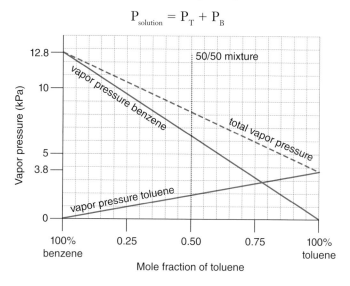

Figure 3-14. *Vapor pressure graph.*

If you start with a 50/50 benzene/toluene mixture, the graph showing vapor pressure/mole fraction relationship (Figure 3-14) indicates that the vapor above the liquid will be richer in benzene than in toluene: the vapor will be ~75 % benzene versus ~25 % toluene. This makes sense, as the boiling point of benzene (80 °C) is lower than the boiling point of toluene (110 °C) at atmospheric pressure. If you record the temperature of the vapor during the distillation of this benzene/toluene mixture, the beginning temperature will be higher than the boiling point of benzene and the end temperature will be lower than the boiling point of toluene, because you are never distilling any pure compound. The temperature profile of the vapor phase for the simple distillation is shown in Figure 3-15.

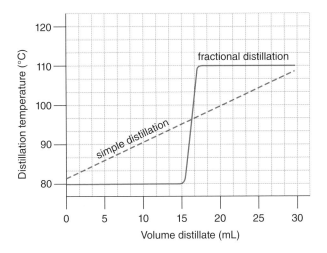

Figure 3-15. *Temperature profile in distillations.*

This example illustrates the limitations of simple distillation. If the boiling points are within 60–70 °C of each other, simple distillation will not result in pure compounds. Organic chemists use simple distillations if the compound is basically pure (>90 % pure) or contains a trace of inorganic non-volatile material, or if one of the components is a solvent with boiling point at least 100 °C lower than the desired compound.

In a simple distillation, the chemical is heated to the boiling point, vaporized and condensed to reclaim the liquid. To accomplish this process a heating source is needed, along with an apparatus to separate the heated vapor from the original liquid, a method to cool the vapor to recondense it, and a vessel to collect the purified liquid. In the laboratory the following six pieces of specialized glassware are used: distilling flask, distillation head, thermometer adapter, water condenser, vacuum takeoff adapter and a receiving flask, as shown in Figure 3-13. The following factors must be taken into consideration when performing a simple distillation:

• The distilling flask should be large enough to easily contain the liquid to be purified. A good rule of thumb is to have a flask whose volume is double the volume of the liquid.

• The distilling flask must be heated and, as discussed in Chapter 1, a variety of heating sources can be used. For a simple distillation, depending on the size and the temperature needed, a heating mantle or a bath containing water (steam), sand or oil are the most common.

• To prevent "bumping" of the liquid, either boiling chips or a stir bar must be used, to provide enough motion in the liquid so that local overheating does not occur.

- The glass joints must be minimally greased to assure a good seal and to avoid the glassware getting stuck, but too much grease will contaminate the sample.

- The thermometer head must be exactly placed in the distillation head to assure accurate measurement of the boiling point.

- Cooling water in the condenser must flow continuously, and should enter the condenser at the bottom and flow out the top so that the condenser is completely filled with water. Depending on the boiling point, regular tap water or cooled ice water can be used. If the boiling point is very high, a water condenser might not be necessary; only air in the condenser will accomplish complete condensation of the hot vapors.

- The vacuum take-off adapter can be left open, or capped with a drying tube if the outside moisture has to be kept away from the distilled liquid. The latter would be necessary if we were drying a solvent to use in a moisture-sensitive reaction. The adapter can also be used to connect to a vacuum source; that will be discussed in more detail below.

- The receiving flask must be tarred before distillation, so accurate yields can be determined. This flask can be cooled in an ice bath if necessary.

- Do not preheat the heating source for your distillation. Lowering a distillation flask in a preheated bath will result in "bumping," and it will also diminish the efficacy of the separation of the different components.

- Never distill the liquid to the point that the distilling flask runs dry. This can lead to accidental overheating of the flask, resulting in the glass breaking, or charring of the last few drops.

Microscale Distillation

Distillation is a very convenient method for purifying a liquid, but because the glassware is fairly large, a certain volume of the compound will be lost. When distilling liters, losing compound doesn't matter much, but for small volumes it becomes a big problem. Different setups attempt to circumvent this problem.

A short path distillation apparatus has a very short condenser, to minimize the losses. Figure 3-16 shows a typical setup which is often sold as a kit. It can be used for simple, fractional, and vacuum distillation and conveniently distills quantities from 5 to 50 mL, but is somewhat expensive.

A simpler version of a short path distillation deletes the condenser completely, and the receiving flask is efficiently cooled in ice water (Figure 3-16). This setup can be used with 100 mL distillation flask, all the way down to a 10 mL round-bottom flask, so very small amounts of liquid can be distilled. This setup cannot effectively be used if the boiling point is too low, because we cannot accomplish very efficient condensation.

A Hickman head can handle both the very small amounts and the low boiling point (Figure 3-16). A Hickman head has a well that collects the distillate and can be equipped with a cooled condenser. Only very small amounts (<2 mL) can be distilled using a Hickman head. The capacity of the head is ~1 mL, but a Hickman head may be purchased with a side arm so that the distillate can be collected during the distillation. A thermometer can be suspended through the condenser to double-check the boiling point. Make sure you do leave the top of the condenser open—never heat a closed system!

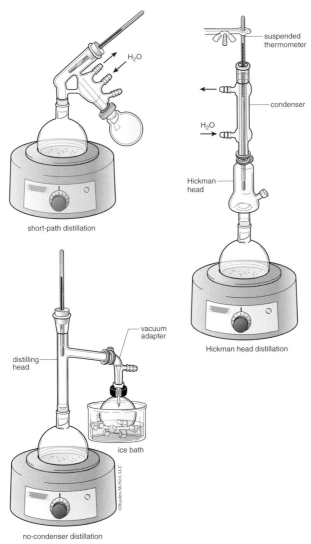

Figure 3-16. *Examples of microscale distillations.*

Fractional Distillation

As shown in Figure 3-14, the composition of the liquid phase is not the same as the composition of the vapor phase if distilling two miscible liquids. If a 50/50 mixture of benzene/toluene is heated to reflux, the vapor contains more benzene than toluene. Therefore, the initial distillate will be richer in benzene than in toluene. The relationship between the composition of the liquid phase and the gas phase is represented by a temperature/composition diagram as shown in Figure 3-17, which roughly represents the case for benzene and toluene.

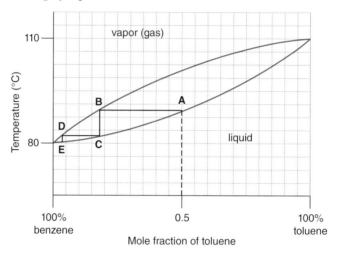

Figure 3-17. *Temperature/composition diagram for fractional distillation.*

When a 50/50 benzene/toluene mixture (A) is heated, the vapor phase will be represented by point B, which upon condensation leads to point C. C has a much higher concentration of benzene, because it is the lower boiling fraction. This is the first fraction that condenses in a simple distillation, and corresponds to a one-plate distillation. However, if solution C is re-vaporized, the vapor obtained corresponds to point D. Upon condensation, point D gives liquid E, which is richer in benzene than C. If this process is continued multiple times, the end result will be pure benzene. Each time the liquid is re-evaporated and re-condensed corresponds to one plate; this is the principle of fractional distillation that employs a long fractionating column, forcing multiple evaporation/condensation cycles before the vapor reaches the top of the column.

Fractional distillation is the experimental procedure used in lab to achieve the separation of two liquids with rather similar boiling points. The experimental setup is basically the same as for a simple distillation, except now a fractionating column is introduced between the distilling flask and the distillation head (Figure 3-18). A multi-head receiver allows collection of different fractions by the simple rotation of this receiver.

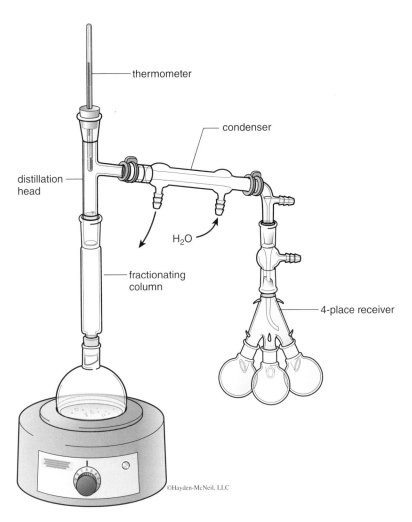

thermometer

condenser

distillation head

H₂O

fractionating column

4-place receiver

©Hayden-McNeil, LLC

Figure 3-18. *Fractional distillation setup.*

A plain fractionating column (shown in Figure 3-18) can be used when it is empty, or it can be filled or packed with suitable materials such as stainless steel sponge or glass beads. The packing allows a mixture to be subjected to many vaporization/condensation cycles as the material moves up the column. With each cycle within the column, the composition of the vapor is progressively enriched in the lower-boiling component. The distillation must be carried out slowly to ensure that numerous vaporization/condensation cycles occur, and that we obtain as pure a product as possible.

Numerous designs for fractionating columns exist, such as the Vigreux and Snyder columns, in which the surface of the columns walls is increased by indentations; the indentations help to form droplets which must then be re-vaporized. A perforated plate column, as shown in Figure 3-19, forces these condensation/evaporation cycles to occur. These columns are often sold with an insulated glass jacket to aid the efficiency of the distillation process. These columns can also be wrapped in aluminum foil so they are protected from the drafts in the laboratory environment.

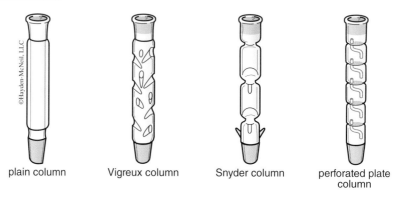

plain column   Vigreux column   Snyder column   perforated plate column

Figure 3-19. *Fractionating columns.*

Vacuum Distillation

Vacuum distillation (distillation at reduced pressure) is used for compounds with high boiling points (above 200 °C); such compounds often undergo thermal decomposition at the temperatures required for their distillation at atmospheric pressure. The boiling point of a compound is lowered substantially by reducing the applied pressure, as illustrated by the phase diagrams (see Chapter 2). Vacuum distillation is also used when it is more convenient to distill at a lower temperature because of experimental limitations, as well as for compounds that, when heated, might react with the oxygen present in air. In the literature, the boiling points will be listed along with the pressure at which the compound was distilled.

It is impossible to calculate the boiling points at reduced pressure, but the boiling point can be estimated. A rule of thumb: the boiling point of many liquids drops about 0.5 °C for every 10 mmHg decrease in pressure when in the vicinity of 760 mmHg. At lower pressures, a 10 °C drop in boiling point is observed for each halving of the pressure.

For a more accurate estimate, a nomograph can be used (Figure 3-20). Let's assume a compound boils at 400 °C at atmospheric pressure (point A). To find the estimated boiling point at 0.2 mmHg (point B), take a ruler and align it so that it passes through both the 400 °C point on the 760 mmHg graph (A) and the

0.2 mmHg on the pressure graph (B). It will intersect the "observed b.p." line at 175 °C (point X), meaning that at 0.2 mmHg its estimated boiling point will be 175 °C.

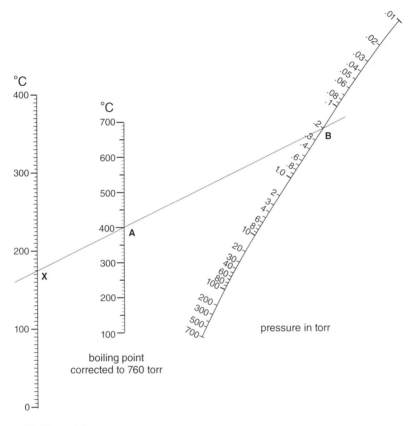

Figure 3-20. *Nomograph.*

A vacuum distillation setup must be able to maintain a vacuum; therefore, it must be completely closed and without leaks. The experimental setup for a vacuum distillation is the same as for a simple distillation, except that a vacuum line is connected to the vacuum adapter (Figure 3-13). The vacuum line is connected to a trap, which in turn is connected to a water aspirator or a vacuum pump. A manometer is often connected to the system to monitor the precise pressure.

Instead of a boiling chip, use a spin bar inside the round-bottom flask. A rapidly spinning spin bar does prevent bumping but a boiling chip will not, since the reduced pressure sucks the trapped air from boiling chips.

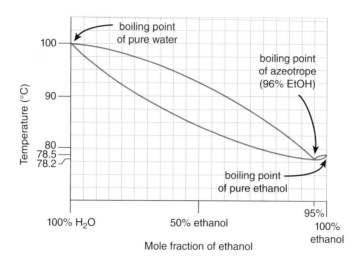

Figure 3-21. *Temperature-composition diagram for an azeotropic distillation.*

Azeotropic Distillation

A completely different situation arises if the two components of a mixture have special interactive forces; in this case, the behavior will deviate from the ideal behavior described above. If a particular composition of the vapor phase is the same as the corresponding liquid phase, azeotropes are formed (Figure 3-21). This results in a constant boiling point and separation becomes hopeless. The azeotrope can be minimum-boiling or maximum-boiling.

A classical example of a minimum-boiling azeotrope is the water/ethanol mixture. The azeotrope boils at 78.6 °C and the composition is 95 % ethanol/5 % water. As seen in the phase diagram shown in Figure 3-21, whichever composition you start with, the azeotropic composition will always distill first. The maximum concentration of alcohol you can obtain from fermentation followed by distillation, therefore, is 95 %, or 190 proof. Absolute ethanol (100 % or 200 proof) cannot be obtained by distillation.

The water/ethanol and water/toluene are the most commonly encountered azeotropes in the organic laboratory. Table 3-2 shows examples of common azeotropes, and a complete listing of known azeotropes can be found in the *CRC Handbook of Chemistry and Physics*.

Table 3-2. Examples of Common Azeotropic Mixtures

Component 1	Component 2	% of Component 2 in the Azeotrope	Boiling Point of the Azeotrope (°C)
Water	Ethanol	96	78.1
Water	Benzene	91	69.2
Water	Toluene	86	84.1
Water	Ethyl acetate	91	70.3
Chloroform	Methyl alcohol	12	53.4
Acetonitrile	Ethyl alcohol	56	72.5

Steam Distillation

When an organic compound is co-distilled with water, it is called steam distillation. The advantage of this technique is that the desired material distills at a temperature below 100 °C (the boiling point of water), even though the compound itself can have a high boiling point.

Why is this so? The laws of physics completely change for immiscible compounds: each component exerts its own vapor pressure, independent of the other components present and independent of the molar fraction. The simple, vacuum, and fractional distillations are applicable to completely soluble (miscible) mixtures only. But when immiscible liquids are distilled, a somewhat different result is observed: the mixture will boil at a lower temperature than the boiling point of any of the separate components as pure compounds. Oils and tars can be steam distilled because they are not miscible with water.

For the steam distillation, the vapor pressure is the sum of the vapor pressures of the pure liquid A and of water, at a given temperature; the molar fractions of the components do not come into play.

$$P_{total} = P_A° + P_{H_2O}° = 760 \text{ mmHg (1 atm)}$$

Because water has the lower boiling point, its vapor pressure at a specific temperature will be large; for example at 99 °C, the vapor pressure of water is 733 mmHg. As a result, compound A will distill in spite of its low vapor pressure, because it will only need a vapor pressure of 27 mmHg at 99 °C to distill. Separation of the distillate will be easy because compound A is insoluble in water.

The setup for a steam distillation is basically the same as for a simple distillation, but to perform a steam distillation, a source of water/steam is needed. Figure 3-22 illustrates two possibilities.

- In the first setup an external source of steam is used: water is heated to boiling in the first flask, and live steam is bubbled through the compound to be distilled. In most cases the heat provided by the steam is sufficient to induce distillation of the mixture out of the second flask, though additional heating might be necessary. The steam mixture is condensed in the water condenser, upon which the organic and aqueous parts separate and the distillate is collected in the receiving flask.

- In the second setup the steam is generated in the same flask as the compound to be distilled. Upon heating, the steam will co-distill with this compound. An addition funnel can be added to the setup, so more water can be added as necessary.

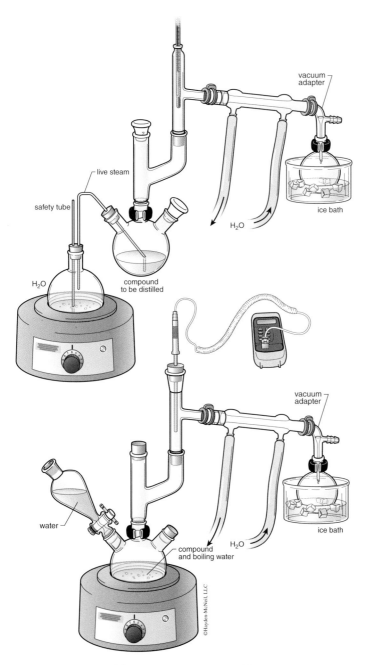

vacuum
adapter

live steam

safety tube

H₂O

ice bath

H₂O

compound
to be distilled

vacuum
adapter

water

ice bath

H₂O

compound
and boiling water

©Hayden-McNeil, LLC

Figure 3-22. *Steam distillation.*

Rotary Evaporation

To evaporate large volumes of solvents in a fast and convenient manner, a rotary evaporator is often used. The full assembly, as seen in Figure 3-23, is commercially available. The solution to be concentrated is placed in the distilling flask, which is connected to the glass joint of the vapor tube. A vacuum is applied, usually 10–20 mmHg, and the distilling flask is rotated. The rotation serves two purposes: it reduces the possibility of "bumping" (although it can still happen), and it greatly increases the surface area of the solution. The solvent will evaporate and condense rapidly on the very dense cooling coil upon which the liquid is collected in the receiving flask. The cooling coil and the receiving flask are often cooled with ice water. The whole assembly is connected to a vacuum source—either a water aspirator or a vacuum pump—and a cold trap is inserted to prevent any non-condensed solvent from contaminating either the water or oil in the pump.

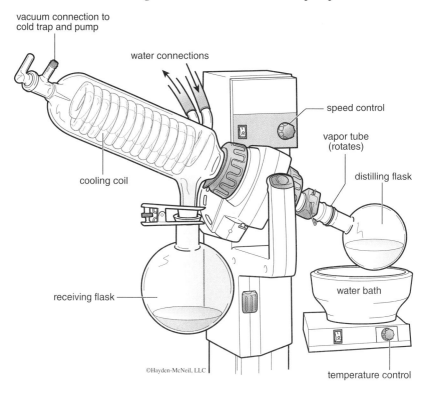

©Hayden-McNeil, LLC

Figure 3-23. *Rotary evaporation.*

The major advantages of rotary evaporation (rotavap) are its speed and efficiency. It is often used in synthetic laboratories to evaporate dilute solutions obtained from extraction procedures or from chromatographic separations.

Here are the steps to follow for a rotary evaporation:

1. Ascertain that the rotavap is clean.

2. Fill the cold trap with a dry ice/acetone or dry ice/isopropanol mixture.

3. Connect to a water aspirator or vacuum pump.

4. Connect the cooling coil to a source of cold or ice water.

5. Pour the solution in the distilling flask, attach the flask to the rotavap, and hold it! Even if you use a clip to hold the flask in place, don't trust it. If you don't support it, it will fall off.

6. Turn on the vacuum, which will keep the distilling flask securely attached. At this point, start the rotation by turning on the motor.

7. Lower the whole assembly in a water bath and start heating.

8. As soon as the pressure is low enough, the solvent will start distilling very quickly.

9. When the distilling flask is "empty" (that is, when it only contains your sample), stop the rotation. Then release the vacuum, take off the distilling flask and place it in a secure location.

10. Empty the receiving flask and trap, and rinse the rotavap if necessary.

Some helpful tips:

•   A bump guard can be inserted between the distilling flask and the tube to prevent excessive bumping. The extent of bumping depends on the solution being distilled.

•   The little plastic clips are convenient to help keep the flask in place, but it will not support the weight of a full flask.

•   Do not preheat the water bath. It will result in bumping when the vacuum is applied.

Sublimation

What Is It Good For?

The inter-conversions of a solid to a gas and from a gas into a solid are both called condensation. Condensation is often used for purification of solids.

The most common example of sublimation in real life is dry ice. The dry ice, which is actually solid carbon dioxide, evaporates as it cools its environment and it evaporates without getting wet, hence its name. In this case only the transformation of solid into gas occurs.

Freeze-dried coffee is another example of the application of the sublimation process. To make freeze-dried coffee, coffee is brewed from coffee beans, then frozen. When placed under vacuum, the water sublimes out of the frozen coffee mixture, leaving behind flakes of easily-dissolved instant coffee. The water from this process is collected as ice in a cold trap.

Another example of sublimation is known to people who live in cold climates. When wet clothes are hung outside in freezing weather, they will freeze solid, but they will still dry. Again, the water sublimes out.

On a Molecular Level

When the vapor pressure of a solid equals the ambient pressure, a solid will sublime. The molecules at the surface of the solid have to be able to escape from the solid phase and transfer into the gas phase. The vaporization is an endotherm process, meaning it takes quite a bit of energy to accomplish the transformation of the solid to the gas phase. As a result, even if external heat is applied to the system, the solid won't melt.

As shown in Figure 3-24, under vacuum and/or with the application of heat, molecules are vaporizing off the surface of the solid; the vapor will sublime back to the solid phase as soon as it comes into contact with a cold surface.

The Basic Principle

Figure 3-25 shows the phase diagram for solid and liquid phases for a substance. Along the solid/gas interphase—the sublimation curve—the solid and vapor are at equilibrium. Along liquid/gas interphase, the liquid and vapor phases are at equilibrium. It is interesting to note that sublimation occurs at lower temperature and at lower pressure than distillation. Also note that both the sublimation temperature and the distillation temperature are highly dependent on the pressure in the system. Sublimation occurs more easily (lower temperature) if the pressure is lowered, just as distillation occurs at lower temperature under vacuum.

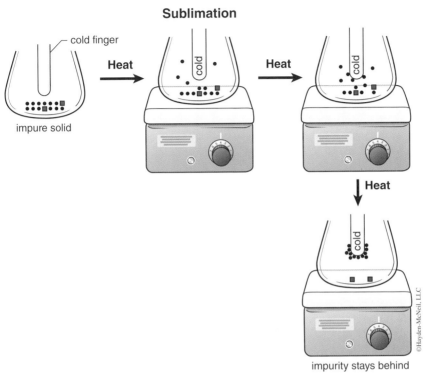

Sublimation

Figure 3-24. *Sublimation.*

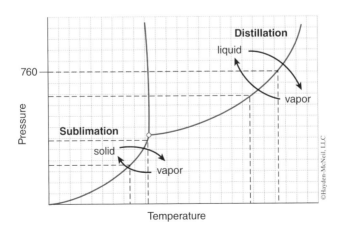

Figure 3-25. *Distillation and sublimation under reduced pressure.*

How Is It Done in the Lab?

Sublimation can be used to purify solids. The solid is warmed until its vapor pressure becomes high enough for it to vaporize, usually with application of vacuum, and the vapor will condense as a solid on a cooled surface placed closely above. This is the basic principle for the experimental setup. The detailed apparatus is mostly dependent on the size, in other words, how much material you are trying to purify by sublimation.

To perform a sublimation, vacuum, cold and heat must be applied in a specific sequence:

1. The first step is to close the system to the outside world by applying the vacuum. This prevents any moisture from entering the system when performing the next step.

2. The cold finger is then filled with an appropriate cold liquid, or connected to a cold re-circulating bath.

3. Heat is then applied to the system, starting the sublimation process.

4. Remove the heat source after the solid has sublimed.

5. The cold source must then be removed, so that no moisture will enter the system after the vacuum is removed.

6. As a last step, the vacuum is carefully released.

In Figure 3-26 some types of apparatus used for sublimation are shown.

- In the simplest setup useful on a small scale, <200 mg, a test tube equipped with a side arm can be used. The cooled condensing surface, called a cold finger, is a tube of smaller diameter that is slightly widened at the appropriate height. The cold finger is held in place with a neoprene filter adapter and filled with ice-cold water. The side arm is connected to a vacuum source, like house vacuum.

- A conical vial and Claisen head, along with a cold finger, can also be used for very small amounts, as shown in the Figure 3-26.

- Commercial glassware is available in many different sizes. The cold finger can be connected either to cold water, a recirculating bath or, when designed for it, filled with a dry ice/acetone mixture. The vacuum source can be either a water aspirator or a vacuum pump.

- Lyophilization or freeze-drying is often used in biochemical applications. In this case, an aqueous solution of the desired compound is frozen before being attached to the lyophilization apparatus, which applies a high vacuum to the flask. The ice stays frozen because the sublimation extracts heat from the solid. After all the ice has sublimed, a nice dry solid stays behind.

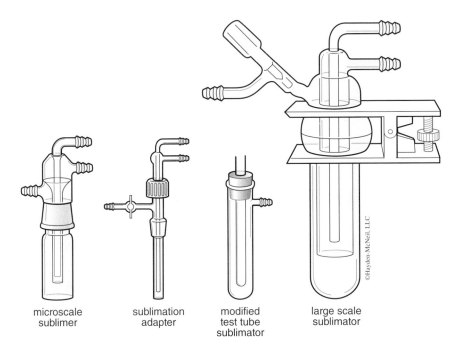

| microscale sublimer | sublimation adapter | modified test tube sublimator | large scale sublimator |

Figure 3-26. *Sublimators.*

Some Practical Tips

- Use the appropriate vacuum source. Low vacuum systems may be used if pressures between 10–100 mmHg are adequate, but a vacuum pump should be used for lower pressures.

- A flame is sometimes the preferred heating device for a sublimation in a research environment, because it is quick and can be applied in a very controlled fashion. However, open flames are usually not allowed in a teaching laboratory environment. Heating mantles and sand baths offer other alternatives.

- Remember that while performing a sublimation, it is important to keep the temperature below the melting point of the solid.

- When collecting material from the cooled surface, carefully remove the central tube (cold finger) from the apparatus to avoid dislodging the crystals that have collected.

- If reduced pressure has been used, the pressure must be released carefully to keep a blast of air from dislodging the crystals.

Chromatography

What Is It Good For?

Chromatography is the separation of a mixture of two or more different compounds or ions by distribution between two phases, one of which is stationary and the other mobile. The principles of chromatography govern such simple methods as thin layer chromatography (TLC) and paper chromatography, as well as highly sophisticated methods such as Gas Chromatography/Mass Spectrometry (GC/MS). The most modern and sophisticated methods of analyzing and separating mixtures that the organic chemist has available today all involve chromatography. One major advantage of chromatography over distillation in these applications, for example, is that it can be performed on a very small scale.

A standard demonstration for elementary school students involves the chromatographic separation of the different dyes in colored pens; to show the students the different components present in these colored pens, paper chromatography in an aqueous medium is performed.

Gas chromatography is used in the analysis of the fat content of foods. How much saturated, unsaturated, and trans fats are there really in your potato chips, or in that container of margarine? These questions can be answered using an analysis involving gas chromatography.

On a Molecular Level

Even though they have different names and the techniques may seem very different, all chromatographic methods work on the same principle. In chromatography, there is always a stationary phase and a mobile phase. The method depends on the differential adsorptivities of the substances to be separated between the two phases. The two most common combinations of phases are liquid/solid and gas/liquid. Separation will be achieved if one component of a mixture adheres more to the stationary phase than the other one.

Various types of chromatography are possible, depending on the nature of the two phases involved:

* Solid-liquid (column, thin layer and paper, high-performance liquid HPLC)

* Gas-liquid (vapor-phase)

* Ion chromatography

In most chromatographic techniques, the stationary phase will be more polar than the mobile phase. In column chromatography, for example, silica gel as the stationary phase is more polar than any organic solvent that can be used as the mobile phase. The exception to this rule is a method called "reverse phase chromatography," in which the stationary phase is less polar and polar solvents such as methanol and water are used as eluent.

Chromatography is based on a partitioning of molecules between a stationary and a mobile phase (Figure 3-27). The basic principles of separation are the same for all different kinds of chromatography. So, as an example, consider a solution containing a mixture of two compounds, which will be introduced on a column. As this solution is placed on the column, each molecule in the solution has to decide if it will stay in the solution (the mobile phase) or adhere to the solid (the stationary phase). The two compounds dissolved in the original solution will have different partitioning factors, meaning that one of them will adhere more to the stationary phase than the other. This partitioning can be governed by a multitude of factors: polarity, solubility in the solvent, hydrogen bonding, volatility in the case of gas chromatography, and so on. A more polar molecule will adhere more strongly to the more polar stationary phase than a less polar molecule.

163

Immediately after the injection all molecules are at the beginning of the column, either in the mobile phase or adhered to the stationary phase. When the mobile phase is pushed through the stationary phase, the molecules will move through the stationary phase at a rate that depends on their different partitioning factors. The molecules that adhere more strongly to the stationary phase will lag behind, while the molecules that do not strongly adhere to this phase will move ahead. Separation is thus achieved. As the mobile phase comes off the column, a detection method must be devised so that you know what comes off when.

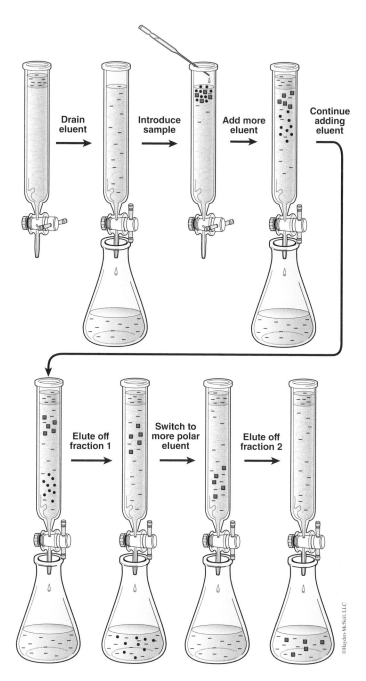

Figure 3-27. *Basic column chromatography.*

Thin Layer Chromatography

Thin layer chromatography (TLC) is very important and convenient for a fast qualitative analysis of a mixture or for very rapid separation of small amounts of material. In TLC, a thin coating of silica gel on a plate of glass is used as the stationary phase, while the moving liquid phase is allowed to climb up the plate. When the bottom end of a coated plate is placed in a solvent, the solvent will creep up the plate due to capillary action. Silica gel (SiO_x) is commonly used for TLC; it is a very fine powder that is highly polar and adheres to the glass. TLC plates with other coatings can be obtained, such as alkaline or acidic alumina or derivatized silica gel.

Thin layer chromatography has several important uses in organic chemistry and, as shown below, can be used in the following applications:

- To establish that two compounds are identical.

- To determine the number of components in a mixture.

- To determine the appropriate solvent for a column-chromatographic separation.

- To monitor a column-chromatographic separation.

- To check the effectiveness of a separation achieved by column chromatography, by recrystallization or by extraction; i.e., how pure is the obtained compound?

- To monitor the progress of a reaction.

- All of these applications can be determined using a minimal amount of material.

As with all chromatographic applications, a normal TLC procedure includes three major steps:

1. **Injection:** for TLC the term "spotting" is used; the sample is applied to the plate before any solvent is allowed to ascend the adsorbent layer.

2. **Separation:** developing or "running" the plate; as the solvent ascends the plate, the sample is partitioned between the moving liquid phase and the stationary solid phase.

3. **Detection:** different methods may be used to visualize the separated spots.

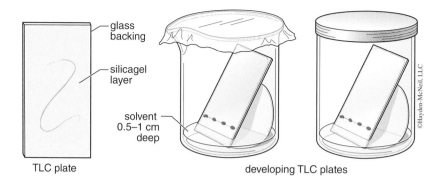

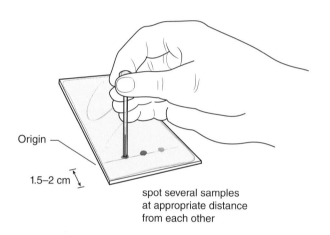

Figure 3-28. *Thin layer chromatography.*

Selecting a TLC Plate

TLC plates are composed of a backing on which an absorbent has been deposited. The most common kind of backing are the silica gel glass plates, which are commercially available, or they can be prepared by dipping two glass plates back-to-back in a slurry of silica gel in a volatile solvent. For most applications, prepared TLC plates are bought commercially. The common size is 5 cm × 10 cm.

Other options include alumina plates, which can be either acidic or alkaline or, for more sophisticated applications, derivatized silica gels are available. The polarity of the absorbent in the latter is controlled by the groups linked to the silica; for example, a long C_{18} chain bonded to the Si–O surface groups will decrease the polarity of the stationary phase.

The backing can be either glass or plastic; in either case, the plates can be precut, or they may need to be cut to an appropriate size. In research labs the plastic-backed plates are very common and, using scissors, are cut into small TLC plates approximately 1 cm by 4 cm.

Spotting

The spot of analyte on the TLC plate should be small and concentrated. To achieve this, specific instructions must be followed (Figure 3-28):

1. Obtain a TLC plate; many are commercially available.

2. Prepare the plate by marking where the spots will be.

    • Use pencil to mark the origin very gently; don't disturb any silica gel particles or make a scratch. Alternatively, you can make tiny scratch marks on the side of the plate. Do not use a pen, as ink will dissolve in the developing solvent.

    • The line should be about 1 cm from the bottom of the plate. The spots must be higher than the level of the developing solvent so that the compounds to be analyzed don't end up in the solvent.

3. Prepare the sample by dissolving it in a chosen volatile solvent (usually acetone or methylene chloride), then place it in a suitable vial.

4. Obtain a capillary tube: they are usually provided as they are commercially available; or prepare one by stretching a glass tube heated in a flame. The diameter of a glass capillary is <0.5 mm.

5. Dip the capillary tube in the solution of sample; it will fill instantly due to capillary action. Empty the solution onto the plate by touching the plate briefly and lightly with the capillary.

6. Keep the spot as small as possible. Ideally, the diameter of the spot should not be larger than 2 mm.

7. The spots must be concentrated enough to be able to see them after development of the plate.

8. Spot multiple times in order to achieve a high concentration of sample in a small spot.

9. Multiple spots can be placed on the line, distributed evenly on the plate to achieve several analyses at the same time. Make sure you know which spot is which, either by marking the plate or by making notes in your notebook.

Developing

The first problem is to choose a developing solvent; the developing solvent used depends on the materials to be separated. The analyte moving up the TLC plate is either in the mobile phase (the solvent) or the stationary phase, and the competition between the two phases determines how fast the different spots will move. More polar solvents will result in higher R_f values and faster movement up the plate.

In the teaching lab, the lab manual will usually tell you which solvent or mixture of solvents to use. This will not be true in a synthetic organic lab, so you have to find the right solvent by trying several different solvents. A solvent that causes all the spotted material to move with the solvent front is too polar, while a solvent that does not create movement in any of the material in the spot is not polar enough.

Some commonly used solvents are:

• Methylene chloride (dichloromethane) and toluene are solvents of intermediate polarity and good choices for a wide variety of functional groups to be separated.

• Hexane(s) and petroleum ether are good choices for hydrocarbon materials.

• Hexane(s) or petroleum ether with varying proportions of toluene or ether gives solvent mixtures of moderate polarity that are useful for many common functional groups.

• More polar materials may require ethyl acetate, acetone, or methanol.

The second problem is to find a container suitable for plate developing (Figure 3-28). The jar must be large enough to contain the plate, though not too large because the atmosphere in the jar has to be saturated with the vapor of the developing solvent, and it must be closed. In the teaching lab a developing jar with a screw cap is often used. Alternatively, a beaker topped with a watch glass is also suitable.

Preparing the developing jar is the next step:

1. Place the appropriate amount of developing solvent into the jar. Pay special attention to the depth of the solvent, as the surface of the solvent should be lower than the spotting line on the plate. Otherwise, the material to be analyzed will dissolve in the developing solvent.

2. Place a filter paper inside the jar as shown in Figure 3-28 and wait until the filter paper is saturated by the solvent. The purpose is to create an atmosphere saturated with the solvent, which will enhance the speed and quality of development of the plate. The filter paper also helps to stabilize the plate.

And now for the development:

1. Place the spotted plate carefully into the jar, then cap the jar.

2. The solvent will start creeping up on the plate due to capillary action. If the atmosphere in the jar is fully saturated, the solvent front will be nice and even.

3. Observe the developing carefully; take out the plate before the solvent reaches the top of the plate.

4. Immediately mark the solvent front (how high the solvent traveled) with a pencil.

5. Be careful never to open the jar during the development, as it will disturb the atmosphere inside the jar and lead to uneven development of the plate.

Visualization

For TLC, the detection of the spots corresponds to visualizing the spots. In some cases, this won't be necessary if the spots are themselves colored and can be seen after developing. But in most cases, the analyzed compounds are colorless and visualization is needed to see the spots and perform the analysis. There are two possibilities: you can either use a visualization method, or you need to modify the spots using a visualization reagent.

Ultraviolet (UV) lamps are used to visualize the spots, either at long or short wavelengths (254 and 366 nm). Place the plate under the lamp and you should be able to see the spots, which you will mark with a pencil. Either the compound in question will fluoresce in UV light and result in a brighter spot than the background, or a fluorescing dye was added to the silica gel and the compound will show up as a darker spot. CAUTION: *Don't look into the lamp as UV rays will harm your eyes.*

If the direct visualization does not work, some simple chemical modification of the spots can be performed to make them visible.

The most often used and simplest visualization reagent is iodine, which reacts with many organic materials to form either brown or yellow complexes. It is most effective if the analytes contain aromatic groups. The iodine is usually kept in a rather large closed jar, so that the atmosphere in the jar is saturated with iodine vapor. Place the developed plate in the jar, cap the jar and shake it for a few seconds until brown or yellow spots appear on the plate. Take the plate out and mark the spots immediately before they disappear, since iodine sublimes easily in air.

The iodine method can be improved by mixing iodine with silica gel, roughly in a 1:10 ratio. This highly increases the surface area available to the iodine and therefore results in much more effective vapor saturation; alternatively, the jar can be heated slightly, resulting in the same effect.

If iodine doesn't work, more sophisticated visualization reagents can be used.

- One option is a solution of potassium permanganate in acidic conditions—it looks like purple juice. The plate is dipped in the solution, then heated on a hot plate on low setting for a few minutes. Ensure that you wipe off the back of the plate before placing it on the hot plate, as the sulfuric acid will damage the surface of the hot plate. After a few minutes brown spots will appear; again, these spots should be marked immediately.

- Anisaldehyde in dilute sulfuric acid solution is especially effective for compounds with carbonyl functionalities.

- Ceric ammonium molybdate in dilute sulfuric acid is effective for hydroxyl compounds.

- Ninhydrin solution is used for amines and amino acids.

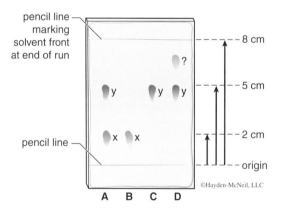

Developed TLC plate
A: Standard containing two components x and y
B: Sample 1 containing x
C: Sample 2 containing y
D: Sample 3 containing y and another, unknown compound

Solvent front at 8 cm—

$$R_f \text{ for } x = \frac{2 \text{ cm}}{8 \text{ cm}} = 0.25$$

$$R_f \text{ for } y = \frac{5 \text{ cm}}{8 \text{ cm}} = 0.625$$

Figure 3-29. *Analyzing several samples.*

Analysis and Applications of TLC

Two major applications of TLC are analyzing a sample and following a reaction. Each will be discussed in detail below.

Each compound placed on a TLC plate will behave in a very specific manner, depending on the conditions of the plate and the experiment: which adsorbent is used, how thick the absorbent layer is and how much of the compound has been spotted, which solvent was used and the ambient temperature. The basic idea is that, under an established set of conditions, a given compound will travel a fixed distance relative to the distance the solvent front travels. The ratio of the distance the compound travels to the distance the solvent travels is called the R_f value, the retardation factor. The R_f value has no units.

$$R_f = \frac{\text{Distance traveled by substance}}{\text{Distance traveled by solvent front}}$$

If two compounds have the same R_f value running side by side on a plate, there is a good chance that these are the same compounds. Conversely, if two compounds have a different R_f value running side by side on the same plate, it is certain that these are different compounds.

Examining Figure 3-29, spot A is a standard containing both x and y; B, C, and D are unknowns. From the TLC plate you can deduce that B contains compound x, C contains compound y, but even though D contains y, it is contaminated with an unknown compound. Calculation of the R_f values reaffirms this diagnosis.

Finally, one of the most important applications of TLC in organic lab is to monitor the progress of a reaction, as illustrated in Figure 3-30. During the period of the experiment, sample the reaction mixture several times and spot on a TLC plate to deduce the following facts:

- Is there still starting material after x minutes?

- Any new compounds present?

- Is there only one product (new material), or do several different new spots show up?

- Does the new spot correspond to the expected product? Does the relative polarity fit the expected structure?

- How long is the optimum reaction time? This means that product is formed in good yield, but no side reactions are interfering yet.

In Figure 3-30, x is the starting material and y is the desired product. After 0.5 hours, the desired product is already present, but not in a large amount. After an additional 0.5 hours, the spot for product becomes better defined while the spot of the starting material starts to fade. After 8 hours, the spot for starting material is totally gone but another spot C appears, which is presumably an unwanted side product. From all this information, it is easy to establish the optimum reaction time; in this case, 5 hours.

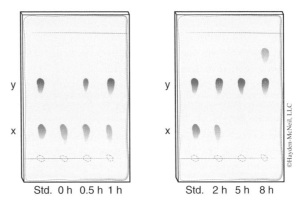

Different spots correspond to different reaction times—
- 0 h Only starting material
- 0.5–5 h More and more product forms and starting material disappears
- 8 h Side reaction leads to product + impurity

Figure 3-30. *Following a reaction.*

Column Chromatography

Column chromatography is a separation technique based on solid-liquid phase partitioning. As the name implies it is run using a column, which can be almost any size, from a small Pasteur pipet to large columns with diameters of 10 cm or more. The stationary phase may be almost any material that does not dissolve in the associated liquid phase; the solids most commonly used are silica gel $SiO_2.xH_2O$ or alumina $Al_2O_3.xH_2O$. These compounds are used in their powdered or finely-ground forms.

To perform a separation using column chromatography, several steps are involved:

1. Selecting a column

2. Selecting a stationary phase and filling the column

3. Selecting eluent(s)

4. Loading the column

5. Running the column

6. Analyzing the eluted fractions

7. Isolating the different components

All these steps will now be discussed in detail.

Selecting a Column

The size of the column depends on the size of the sample to be separated or purified, as well as on the difference in R_f values of the different components. For a very small sample with good separation, a column as small as a Pasteur pipet can be used. With more sample, or with a mixture which will be difficult to separate, a larger column will be chosen. The diameter of the column will be related to the amount of sample, while the length of the column will depend on the difficulty of the separation. Use the smallest and shortest possible column to achieve the necessary separation. It will save time, packing material, and solvent (Figure 3-31).

Generally, the total weight of absorbent used should be about 20 times the weight of the crude sample. So for a small sample, 100–200 mg, only about 2–3 g of absorbent will be sufficient, while a 20 g sample will require a large column containing ~250 g of absorbent.

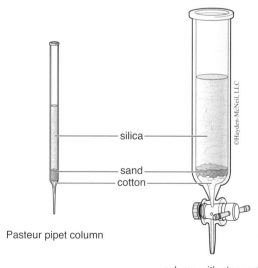

silica

sand

cotton

Pasteur pipet column

©Hayden-McNeil, LLC

column with stopcock

Figure 3-31. *Microscale and macroscale chromatography columns.*

In addition to the size of the column, other practical decisions have to be made.

- The first decision is how to control the elution rate of the column. As the solvent runs through the column from top to bottom, it is advantageous to be able to decide how fast to run the column. Simple columns have a stopcock at the bottom. A more primitive approach consists of a piece of rubber tubing on the bottom that is clamped down to either slow or completely stop the flow rate.

- The absorbent consists of a fine powder, and therefore a support is necessary to keep the absorbent from flowing out of the column. A plug of cotton or glass wool is pushed to the bottom of the column and covered with a thin layer of sand. When using a Pasteur pipet column, a very small plug of cotton is placed in the narrow area at the bottom of the pipet. The only role this cotton plug plays is to keep the absorbent in the column. Don't pack the cotton too tightly or it will form a plug and the column won't drain.

Filling the Column

The next decision is to select an absorbent. Powdered or finely-ground alumina or silica gel can be used. Activated alumina is sold as powders—it can be neutral, basic or acidic, pH ~7, 10 or 4, respectively. "Activated" means that it has been heated to high temperature and almost all water has been removed. Silica gel, on the other hand, contains about 10–20 % of water. The hydroxyl-groups of silica gel can be functionalized with different non-polar groups, such as long C_{18} chains or slightly more polar $-CH_2CH_2CN$ chains; in this case the stationary phase becomes less polar than the eluent, and the technique is called *reverse phase chromatography*.

The size of particles is also important. If they are too small, the separation will be very good but the solvent will drain very slowly. On the other hand, if the size of the particles is too large, the column will drain very effectively but the separation might be compromised. The most common silica gel used is "Silica gel 60," 70–230 mesh (63–200 µm particle size), which corresponds to a surface area of ~500 m^2/g.

A column can be filled by either the dry or wet packing method.

- Dry packing method: For very small columns, such as a Pasteur pipet, the column can be filled with dry absorbent. Place some absorbent on a weighing paper folded in half and slowly fill the column. The side of the column is tapped to ascertain that the powder is nicely packed in the column. The organic solvent selected as eluent is added to the column to saturate the absorbent.

- Wet packing method: A more common technique is to fill a column using the slurry method. The absorbent is mixed with an organic solvent in a beaker to form a slurry; the slurry should have the consistency of a thick batter, but still flow. This slurry is then poured into the column using a funnel, with the stopcock at the bottom of the column open to allow the excess solvent to drain out. The sides of the column are tapped to remove any air bubbles from the slurry. Continue adding the slurry until the desired height of absorbent is achieved.

- Once a column is filled, it should never be allowed to run dry; if the absorbent is allowed to dry in certain spots, the homogeneity of the column is compromised. Cracks can develop in the body of the column or between the absorbent and the glass wall of the column, which will adversely affect the separation.

- After running the column, the absorbent can be easily removed by holding the column upside down, opening the stopcock and slightly tapping the side of the column. Make sure you dispose of the absorbent responsibly.

Selecting Eluent

The choice of eluent is extremely important to achieve effective separation. The eluent is selected by doing test runs on TLC plates. The stationary phase of the TLC plate must match the absorbent used in the column as closely as possible; a silica gel TLC is used if silica gel will be the column packing.

The more polar the analyte, the more polar the eluent should be. For example, a plant extract contains both carotene and xanthophyll, and has therefore been placed on the column (Figure 3-32). Carotene is very non-polar; there are basically no attractive forces between the carotene molecules and polar stationary phase. It will therefore easily elute off the column using very non-polar eluent such as hexanes. The xanthophyll, on the other hand, is more polar (has two hydroxy groups) and will "stick" to the column; it will more strongly adhere to the polar stationary phase. A more polar solvent (or solvent mixture), such as hexanes/acetone in a 80/20 ratio, will be needed to elute it off the column.

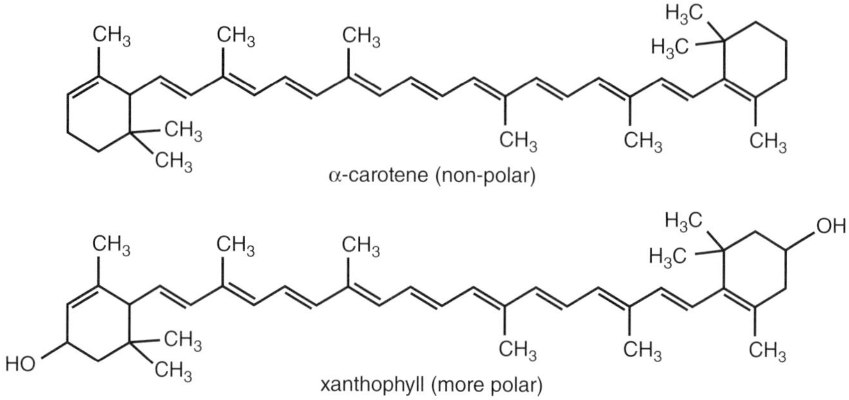

Figure 3-32. *Examples of polar and non-polar analytes.*

To effectively separate different components of a mixture, a difference in R_f value of at least 0.2 is necessary. In this case one eluent mixture can be used to run the complete separation; alternatively, you can switch solvents during the run of the column: once one component has eluted, a more polar solvent is introduced on the column to elute the next component. For this purpose, mixtures of non-polar and more polar solvents are very effective, because the elution rate of the different fractions can be precisely fine-tuned.

For a solvent to be useful in column chromatography, it should be readily available, inexpensive, relatively non-toxic and with a boiling point between 50 and 120 °C. The boiling point should be high enough so that while running the column, rapid evaporation is not a problem, but the solvent should also be easily removed by rotary evaporation after the fractions are collected. Listed in approximate order of increasing polarity, the following solvents are very commonly used for column chromatography:

- very non-polar: from hydrocarbons (hexanes, cyclohexane, and petroleum ether) to toluene and carbon tetrachloride

- slightly polar: diethyl ether, dichloromethane, and chloroform

- polar: acetone and ethyl acetate

- very polar: ethanol and methanol

Loading the Column

Loading the column means placing the mixture to be separated on the packing material.

- The mixture to be separated is dissolved in a minimal amount of the eluent. A less polar solvent can also be used.

- This analyte is loaded on the column using the following procedure: First, the eluent is eluted from the column by opening the stopcock until the eluent level exactly matches the level of the absorbent; no solvent remains on top of the absorbent. Then the analyte solution is carefully placed on top of the absorbent without disturbing the top layer of the absorbent; a syringe or a Pasteur pipet can be used to accomplish this.

- The stopcock is slowly opened to allow the solution to be absorbed on the column; the column is drained until the liquid level exactly matches the top of the absorbent.

- The organic compound will adsorb onto or adhere to the fine particles of the absorbent. If the solution is colored, a colored band should be visible at the top of the column.

- More eluent can now be added to start running the column.

Running the Column (Figure 3-27)

- Eluent is continuously added to the column. The elution rate is controlled by the stopcock.

- As the different fractions are eluted off the column, the polarity of the eluent can be gradually increased. Either pure solvents of increasing polarity or mixtures of solvents containing a larger fraction of the more polar component can be used to accelerate the elution of the different fractions.

- At the bottom of the column, different fractions are collected: either the elution of the different components is monitored (this is possible in the case of brightly-colored compounds) and a new fraction is collected every time a component elutes. A new fraction may also be started every time a specific volume has eluted off the column.

- The fractions are collected manually, or the column can be placed above a fraction collector. The latter consists of an array of test tubes on a platform. The platform is shifted slightly after a set time interval, and the next test tube is placed underneath the column. Make sure to label the different fractions.

- The most common method used to analyze the different fractions is to run TLC plates on either all the fractions, or on selected fractions. The TLC plates will reveal in which fractions the different components of the mixture are.

- Based on the analysis of the TLC plates, different fractions can be combined if they contain the same component of the mixture. After evaporation of the solvent, the different components are isolated and can be further purified.

Other Column Chromatography Methods

Flash Chromatography

Column chromatography has its limitations, the major one being that it is slow: it relies on gravity to move the eluent down the column and the particle size of the stationary phase cannot be too small, otherwise the solvent won't drain. Better separation could be achieved if the absorbent particles were smaller, because this would increase the total surface area of the stationary phase; however, this really slows down the elution rate considerably.

One technique used to speed up the chromatography process is to exert air pressure on the column, which forces the eluent to elute faster; this is called *flash chromatography*. One method is to cap a regular column so that the system is closed, then connect it to a gas cylinder with compressed air; the applied pressure determines the elution rate. Another method is to buy pre-packed silica gel cartridges, which are used in a system not unlike a gas chromatography setup, complete with an injection port and detector.

When using a Pasteur pipet as the column, flash chromatography can be mimicked by exerting pressure on the "column" with a rubber bulb. This will push the eluent out of the column faster, but the flow rate cannot be controlled, nor is it constant in this setting. Care should also be taken not to "suck up" the stationary phase when refilling the bulb with air.

High Performance Liquid Chromatography (HPLC)

The analysis of organic mixture can be greatly improved by using very fine absorbent and commercially-packed columns. The smaller the particle size of the absorbent, the larger the surface area. However, this small particle size makes it extremely difficult to pass eluent through the column. As shown in flash chromatography, pressure will speed up the analysis. In HPLC extremely high pressure can be used—as high as 1,000 psi. The columns are made of steel, and expensive pumps are used to achieve these pressures. HPLC systems are sold commercially and can be very sophisticated.

The columns have a small diameter, but extremely good separation is achieved because of the small particle size. The analyses can be run on an analytical scale, using small columns and fast analysis; alternatively, semi-preparative and preparative systems can be used to separate pure materials on a large enough scale to isolate the materials.

The analysis is usually run on extremely small amounts, and specific detectors are used to analyze the mobile phase as it comes off the column. Different detection methods are:

- UV, which is very sensitive and easy to use, but the compounds must absorb in the UV region.

- RI, refractive index detector, which measures the variations in refractive index of the eluted fractions. It is a universal detector, but it is very temperature-sensitive and difficult to obtain a stable baseline.

- Fluorescence detector is very sensitive and selective, but the analyte has to have a fluorophore group.

- MS (mass spectral) detector, which is expensive, extremely sensitive and gives information about the structure of the analyte as it elutes off the column.

Supercritical Fluid Chromatography (SFC)

Above the critical temperature T_c a vapor can no longer be converted to a liquid, independent of the pressure. This is called a supercritical fluid. These fluids have densities comparable to liquids but their viscosities are very low, like gases.

A prime example of a supercritical fluid is supercritical carbon dioxide, which has a critical temperature of 31.3 °C. Above this temperature, it can be used as a "solvent" for reactions or in chromatographic applications. Supercritical CO_2 is currently also used as a green dry cleaning solvent.

The instrumentation for SFC is very similar to HPLC, except that in the case of supercritical fluids, both the pressure and temperature must be controlled.

Gas Chromatography

All the chromatographic methods discussed above have a solid stationary phase and a liquid mobile phase. In gas chromatography, the stationary phase is liquid and the mobile phase is a gas. The liquid stationary phase is a high boiling organic compound adsorbed on the solid inert packing in the column. In classical gas chromatography, the columns are steel. The column is placed in an oven, which offers temperature control.

Gas chromatography is one of the most useful instrumental tools for separating and analyzing organic compounds that can be vaporized without decomposition. Separation is based on a combination of volatility of the components of a mixture and the differing polar interactions with the stationary phase. A carrier gas (usually helium, argon, or nitrogen) flows through the column, but does not interact significantly with the analyte on a molecular level. The mixture of compounds to be separated is introduced into the carrier gas stream, where its components are equilibrated (or partitioned) between the moving gas phase and the stationary liquid phase.

The major applications of gas chromatography are:

•   test the purity of a substance and separate the components of a mixture;

•   determine the relative amount of the components in a mixture;

•   identify a compound;

•   as preparative method to isolate pure compounds from a small amount of a mixture.

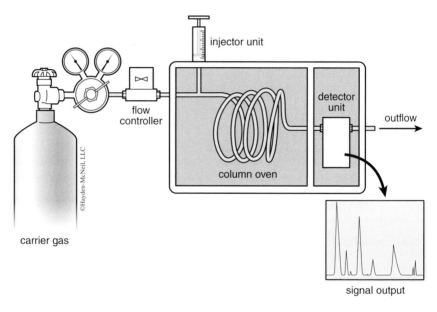

Figure 3-33. *Gas chromatography.*

Gas Chromatography Setup

A gas chromatograph, or GC, consists of many different components. Figure 3-33 shows the basic setup, which consists of

- a gas cylinder containing the carrier gas with a flow controller attached;

- an injector port, which is temperature-controlled;

- a column in a temperature-controlled oven;

- a temperature-controlled detector;

- a recorder or other signal output device.

Selecting a Column

The first decision to make is to select a column; both the size and the packing can be varied. Columns come in two major varieties: packed columns and glass capillary columns.

A *packed column* is made of steel tubing. A typical size is 2–4 mm inner diameter and the length can vary between 1–3 m. The packing consists of an inert solid support, which is coated with a non-volatile liquid. The effectiveness of the column is determined by this liquid component. The packing of the column is selected based on the components to be injected. The liquid component can interact with the compounds being analyzed by dipolar interactions, hydrogen bonding, Van der Waals forces, or even specific interactions between functional groups. A decision as to which kind of column to use can be made by consulting catalogs listing which mixtures can be separated on which columns. Typical columns are:

- **Carbowax columns:** the liquid phase is polyethylene glycol (polar, contains OH groups) and it is used to separate carboxylic acids and alcohols.

- **SE-30 columns:** the liquid phase is polydimethyl siloxane (non-polar) and is very useful in the separation of such non-polar analytes as hydrocarbons, polycyclic aromatics, PCBs, and steroids.

- **SE-52 columns:** the liquid phase is poly(phenylmethyl dimethyl) siloxane (non-polar) which is commonly used in FAME analyses (fatty acid methyl esters), and also for halogenated compounds.

Some of these packings are more temperature stable than others, and the maximum operating temperature must always be taken into account. The typical temperature range for a column is either up to 250 °C or up to 350 °C.

Gas chromatography can also be used for *preparative* purposes; in this case, the components of the mixture are physically separated and collected at the end of the column. For preparative gas chromatography, very large columns can be used; for example, up to 10 m in length. These days preparative GC has been largely displaced by preparative HPLC methods.

The second type of column is the *capillary column*, which is a very long, thin glass capillary tube. The inner diameter of a glass capillary column is less than 1 mm and it can be several meters in length. The liquid stationary phase is now spread out on the inside of this capillary tube. Quite good separations are achieved with capillary gas chromatography, but only very small amounts of solution can be injected. Because these columns provide much better separation than packed columns, they are the first choice for analytical purposes.

The Carrier Gas

The nature of the carrier gas is determined by the detection method, as well as the price. The carrier gas must be inert; it doesn't interact with the analyte, it merely serves to push the molecules through the column. Helium is the first choice because it is non-polar and readily available.

The flow rate of the carrier gas will determine how fast the sample will move through the column. The flow rate can be fixed on the GC itself, but the accuracy should occasionally be checked with a flow meter. A flow meter can be as simple as a glass tube with some soap solution in a rubber bulb at the bottom. The gas is led into the tube and the flow rate can be observed by how fast the soap bubbles migrate up the column. High flow rates will minimize the amount of time the molecules spend in the stationary phase, thereby adversely affecting the separation. If the flow rate is too slow, the analysis will take too long and the separation won't be as effective because the molecules could actually migrate backwards.

Injection

A crucial component of a gas chromatograph is the injection port. Using a microliter syringe, the sample is introduced onto the column either as an undiluted liquid or as a solution. The sample is injected through a rubber septum into a heated chamber called the injection port. The temperature of the injection port has to be high enough to immediately vaporize the complete injection volume; this is essential for good separation. All molecules must start the separation process at exactly the same time; as in column chromatography, the complete sample is placed as tightly as possible at the beginning of the column. The injection port is usually between 250 and 300 °C to make sure everything immediately vaporizes.

The sample is injected through a rubber septum, which is necessary to keep all the injected material inside the GC and to maintain the positive pressure inside the column. The rubber septum is perforated every time a sample is injected. After a certain number of injections, the rubber septum will start to wear out and holes may form; the rubber septum should then be replaced.

The Microliter Syringe (Figure 3-34)

Microliter syringes are used because the injected sample size has to be carefully controlled. The needle has a very small gauge, which minimizes the damage done to the septum with each injection. Too much sample overloads the column and results in very poor separation, while too little sample will adversely affect the detection at the end of the column. Microliter syringes are expensive and very delicate, and should be treated with great care.

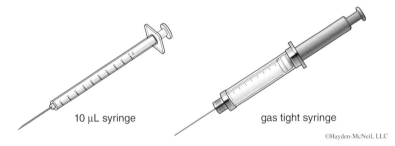

10 μL syringe   gas tight syringe

©Hayden-McNeil, LLC

Figure 3-34. *Syringes.*

The very small gauge needle can easily become clogged, and it is therefore essential that the syringe is rinsed out immediately after every use. A small bottle of acetone or ether is usually kept near the GC. After injection, a small amount of the solvent is pulled into the syringe and expelled several times, to remove all remaining traces of the injected compound. This will also prevent cross-contamination of the samples.

The plunger on a microliter syringe is made of a chemically resistant alloy, but it can be bent. Once the plunger is bent, it makes the syringe unusable; therefore, great care must be taken so that the plunger is pushed without bending.

For injection of gases, gas tight syringes can be provided. Simple plastic syringes can also be used for injection of gases, but for accurate measurements the gas tight syringes must be used. These syringes are larger in volume because they are used only to inject gases.

Detection

The different components of the mixture have to be detected as they come off the column. Because they are in the gas phase, the concentration of the components is extremely low. The detector must be very sensitive and its temperature very high, to keep the sample from condensing at this point. The detector temperature is often 300 °C.

The simplest detection method for gas chromatography is thermal conductivity detection (TCD). The eluting gas passes over a wire and if the gas contains anything besides the carrier gas, a spike in conductivity will be registered. These peaks are recorded using a chart recorder or a computer. TCD is simple and inexpensive, but not very sensitive.

A more sensitive detector is a flame ionization detector (FID). The gas stream eluting from the column is led through a continuously burning hydrogen flame placed between two electrodes, while oxygen is also fed into the detector to assure effective burning. When an organic compound elutes off the column and enters the flame, most of the molecules will be burned; that is, they will form CO_2 and H_2O. However, a small portion of the molecules will ionize. These ions will be trapped by the electrode and a signal sent to the detector. FID is very sensitive, but it destroys the sample.

Other detection methods for GC exist; the most widely used of these is GC/MS, in which the detector is a mass spectrometer and immediately generates information about the structure of the eluted compounds.

Running the GC

Setting the parameters:

The temperature settings of the injector, column oven and detector have to be selected. Both the injector and detector have to be at very high temperature, so they will be heated to at least 250 °C.

The oven temperature will directly affect the separation. If set too high, the different components will elute too fast, and no separation will be observed. If set too low, the peaks start to broaden and the analysis will be too long. The oven temperature must always be below the maximum temperature reported for the liquid stationary phase. If the temperature is higher than the specified temperature maximum, the liquid phase will start to bleed off the column. Trial and error will determine the optimum temperature, but a good starting point is 10–20 °C below the boiling point of the mixture.

The flow rate of the carrier gas must also be set. For packed columns, a flow rate of 60–70 mL/min is common; the same flow rate can be used for capillary columns. Lower flow rates are advisable for longer packed columns or for smaller diameter columns.

The GC analysis:

Injection of the sample must be clean and accurate, so proper injection technique is essential. The syringe is filled with the sample and held with two hands—one hand on the syringe body while the other hand holds the plunger in place—and is then firmly inserted through the septum. If the plunger is not held, the larger pressure inside the column can push the plunger out. Make sure the syringe is inserted straight through the septum, otherwise it could miss the column entirely.

The exact time of injection must be recorded. Some GCs will have a button you can push that sends a signal to the recorder. If not, mark the exact time on the recorder with either a pencil mark or by turning the base line knob on the recorder up and down. Another method is to inject a small air bubble with the sample: pull the syringe back a bit once it is filled. The air will create a small blip in the chromatogram and is used as a reference.

As the mixture reaches the column, the different components of the mixture will begin to equilibrate between the liquid and gas phases. The length of time required for a sample to move through the column is a function of how much time it spends in the vapor phase and how much time it spends in the liquid phase. The more time it spends in the vapor phase, the faster it gets to the end of the column. In most separations, the components of a sample have rather similar solubilities in the liquid phase. Therefore, the time the different compounds spend in the vapor phase is mostly a function of their vapor pressure, and the more volatile component arrives at the end of the column first.

Several factors affect the separation:

- The boiling point of compounds: Compounds with lower boiling points generally travel through the gas chromatograph faster than compounds with higher boiling point. This is because low-boiling compounds always have higher vapor pressures than compounds with a higher boiling point.

- The flow rate of the carrier gas: The carrier gas must not move so rapidly that molecules of the sample in the vapor phase cannot equilibrate with the liquid phase. If the rate of flow is too slow the bands broaden significantly, leading to poor resolution and difficulty in the chromatograph analysis.

- The choice of liquid phase used in the column: The molecular weights, functional groups, and polarities of the component molecules in the mixture to be separated will help determine the choice of the packing of the column.

Analysis of the Gas Chromatogram

The end result of a gas chromatographic run is a gas chromatogram (Figure 3-35). The gas chromatogram will look the same, independent of the detection method and independent of the recording device, namely peaks with different intensities placed on the x-axis which corresponds to time. The position of the peak corresponds to the retention time; i.e., how much time this particular component stayed on the column. The chromatogram can be recorded on a simple chart recorder, on a computer or using an integrator, which gives you immediate feedback about the position and size of the peaks.

The injection time is indicated on this chart, as well as the peaks as they elute off the column. The surface of the peaks roughly corresponds to the amount of the different components. The position of the peaks relative to the injection point in GC can be used for two main purposes: to assess the purity of a compound and to identify the components of a mixture.

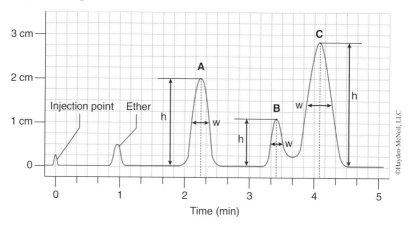

	Retention time	Area (h × w/2)
A	2.25 min	2 cm × 0.5 cm = 1.0 cm²
B	3.45 min	1.1 cm × 0.25 cm = 0.275 cm²
C	4.1 min	2.8 cm × 0.7 cm = 1.96 cm²

Figure 3-35. *Analysis of a gas chromatogram.*

Just as R_f values in TLC yield information about the identity of a certain compound, so too the retention times in GC. If the parameters of a GC are unchanged, two separate analyses yielding peaks with the same retention time will lead to the conclusion that these two compounds may indeed be the same. We can prove that two compounds are different if they have different retention times, but keep in mind that two different compounds may have the same retention time. As with many analysis methods, you can only prove a negative with GC.

The identity of a component of a mixture can be further evaluated by spiking the injection mixture with a small amount of the known component. In this case, the corresponding peak in the chromatogram will be larger. Standards are routinely used in gas chromatography to help in the identification of compounds.

To completely identify this compound, it will have to be isolated and analyzed by spectroscopic methods such as IR and NMR.

Quantitative Analysis:
A gas chromatogram yields valuable information about the composition of a volatile mixture. Comparing several chromatograms will yield information about the relative amounts of different components in a mixture. To get accurate information, a calibration must be performed. To achieve this, known quantities of known compounds are injected, and these quantities are then compared to the surface of the corresponding peaks.

Quite a bit of information can be collected from a GC without going through the trouble of constructing a calibration curve. Let's assume that the detector's responses to the different components of a mixture are roughly the same. Now the peak surface can be used as a direct measure of the amounts of the different components.

Most peaks approximate the shape of an isosceles (symmetrical) triangle. The surface of the triangle is equal to one half of the base multiplied by the height. But in a chromatogram it is often difficult to measure the base; the width at half-height is a more dependable measurement, so the surface of the triangle is equal to the width at half-height times the height (Figure 3-35).

Internal normalization can be used to calculate the percentage composition of a mixture, meaning that the total surface of all the peaks is assumed to correspond to 100 %. The percentage of component A in the chromatogram shown in Figure 3-35 can be calculated from the area of peak A divided by the total area of peaks A + B + C, multiplied by 100 %.

Total area = area peak A + area peak B + area peak C = 3.235 cm^2

% A = (area peak A/total area) × 100 % = (1.0/3.235) × 100 % = 31 %

Integrators and computers used as output devices to generate the chromatogram will automatically generate the percentage area for each peak, making the above calculations unnecessary.

Problems for Chapter 3

1. Anita Z. weighed out 220 mg of impure sucrose. After recrystallization from water, Anita obtained 235 mg of solid compound. What happened? How can this be corrected?

2. Jack weighed 100 mg impure salicylic acid. After recrystallization from ethyl acetate, he obtained only 22 mg. Where is the remainder? How can Jack increase the yield?

3. Explain how you would separate the following mixtures using acid/base extraction:

   a. Benzoic acid and *t*-butylbenzene
   b. Triethylamine and *p*-dichlorobenzene
   c. Pyridine and octanoic acid

4. The partition coefficient for compound A between hexanes and water is 12. Assume 10 g of A is dissolved in 100 mL of water. This aqueous solution is extracted with 100 mL of hexanes. How much A will the first hexanes fraction contain? How about a second extraction with another 100 mL of hexanes?

5. Propanoic acid is reacted with hexanol in acidic conditions, i.e. a few drops of sulfuric acid, to form the ester hexyl propanoate. Excess propanoic acid is used to obtain a high yield. Work-up of the reaction starts with extraction using aqueous sodium bicarbonate and diethyl ether, followed by extraction with water. The ether layer is dried using magnesium sulfate, filtered and evaporation of the solvent. Write out all the reactions which will happen in the extraction steps. Then draw a flow diagram depicting how pure ester product will be obtained from these extractions.

6. Draw a flow diagram to separate the following compounds by extraction: aniline, benzoic acid, and acetophenone.

7. Stacey adds so much $MgSO_4$ to an ether solution of hexyl propanoate that no liquid can be seen anymore. How can Stacey recover her product?

8. Compounds A and B have boiling points of 120 and 180 °C, respectively. Joan distills the mixture nice and slowly, while John rushes through the distillation really fast because he wants to get out of lab early. Who will have the purest compounds, and why?

9. Consider the following pairs of compounds. For which pairs can simple distillation be used, and for which ones would fractional distillation be more suitable? (You will have to look up the boiling points.)

   a. Hexyl acetate and butyl acetate
   b. Hexanol and cyclopentanol
   c. *p*-Xylene (1,4-dimethylbenzene) and benzene

10. Using the nomograph in Fig. 3-20, estimate the following boiling points:

    a. *p*-Xylene (bp 138 °C at 760 mm) at 150 mmHg
    b. *p*-Xylene at 15 mmHg
    c. Linoleic acid (230 °C at 16 mmHg) at atmospheric pressure

11. A mixture of compounds A and B was run on TLC using 10% ethyl acetate/90% hexanes, and the R_f values of 0.05 and 0.12 were obtained. Is this optimal? How can the separation be improved?

12. A mixture of phenol and cyclohexanol is run on a TLC plate using 30% ethyl acetate/70% hexanes. Only one spot is seen using a UV lamp. Does this mean that both compounds have the same R_f? How can the problem be solved?

13. Assume that compounds A and B have R_f values of 0.3 and 0.5, respectively. How far will each of these compounds travel if the solvent front reaches 8 cm?

14. A mixture of *p*-methylstyrene, *p*-methoxystyrene and *p*-cresol (*p*-methylphenol) is run, and the following spots are obtained.

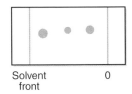

Solvent   0
front

Calculate the R_f values and match the three compounds to the three spots.

15. In which order would the following compounds elute on a silica gel column using hexanes/ethyl acetate as eluent?

16. Janet is planning on separating the components of an extract obtained from tomatoes. The instructions in her lab manual told her to first use hexanes as an eluent, followed by a 50/50 mixture of hexanes and acetone, and finally pure acetone. Janet however did exactly the exact opposite. What would be the outcome?

17. A mixture of benzene, toluene, and xylene is injected on a gas chromatography column. The following gas chromatogram is obtained. What was the composition of the injected sample?

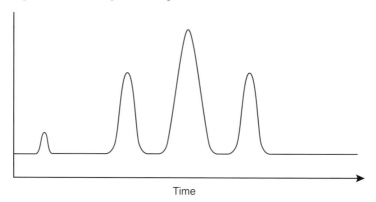

Time

Running a Reaction

4

Setup

Preparations before carrying out the reaction:

- Check the literature. Rely on what other scientists have done before you.

- Outline the whole reaction, including how you are going to isolate the product and purify it.

- Decisions must be made as to the scale of reaction and which equipment to use. Do the necessary calculations; decide on appropriate reagents and solvents, reaction temperature, etc.

- Calculate the total volume of the reaction, and use a flask with at least twice that capacity. Locate a clean, dry flask, a stir bar, a septum and any other glassware necessary for the procedure.

- If the reaction is moisture- or air-sensitive, oven- or flame-dry the flask and other glassware. Prepare to run the experiment under an inert atmosphere.

- Purify reagents and solvents, if necessary.

- Locate syringes and needles of appropriate size, if necessary.

- Weigh the reactants. Consult the procedure to see what is necessary. Do not mix anything yet, and do not weigh sensitive reagents until just before use.

Execution of the Reaction

How to run the reaction, from start to end, and how to monitor reaction progress.

- Always save a small sample of each reactant for TLC and NMR comparison.

- Follow the literature procedure exactly. Unless you are familiar with the reaction, don't make any changes when running the reaction for the first time.

- Spot a sample of the reaction on TLC as soon as the reaction is started. Co-spot with your reactant sample(s).

- Record all observations and times in the notebook.

- Label the reaction. It is also necessary that your lab mates know what you are doing; talking in lab is a good thing!

- Follow the reaction by TLC, or GC or any other method if appropriate, at regular intervals. The appropriate interval depends on the expected reaction time.

- Never leave the lab when a reaction is running unless you put somebody else in charge.

- When one of the reactants has been consumed, stop the reaction immediately.

- Quench the reaction (stop the reaction) in the recommended fashion. This can be cooling the reaction mixture, or pouring in water, or...

- If gas is evolved during the quench, or if it is exothermic, watch the reaction carefully to be sure it is under control. Patience is highly recommended.

The Workup

Isolating the products from reagents and solvent.

- Extraction is the most common type of workup.

- The first step can be either pouring the reaction mixture in water (ice if necessary) or diluting the reaction mixture with an appropriate solvent.

- The product will usually be in the organic layer. It must be washed with various aqueous solutions. In the original plan for the reaction, you should have an extraction scheme to remove all unwanted products.

- Remember: don't dispose of any of the extraction fractions until you are sure that you have your entire product.

- Dry the organic layer.

- Remove the solvent by rotoevaporation.

- The crude product is now ready for primary identification.

Primary Identification

Did you really make what you thought you wanted to make and how do you proceed?

- Run a TLC of the crude product to make sure you have what you think you have. If an authentic sample of the product is available, spot it also on the TLC plate.

- Run spectra on the crude sample: NMR, IR, GC/MS, ... It is important to know what else is in the crude reaction mixture. How much starting material is still present? How much byproduct has been formed? Spectra on crude products will also give information about minor components formed during the reaction: Did other isomers, decomposition products, polymeric products form during the reaction?

- If unexpected products are observed, decide if they are important or not. Can their formation be avoided? Or maybe they are interesting and present another angle to the research?

- Decide at this point if you want to proceed to purification and final identification, or start again with a different plan.

Purification and Final Identification

How are you going to purify the compound? And complete structure identification.

- Decide on a purification method. Should the compound be recrystallized? Or distilled? Or do you run a column?

- How will you know if it is really pure?

- Repeat purification if necessary.

- Run detailed spectra: proton and carbon NMR, GC/MS (will show residual volatile impurities), IR.

- Submit for high resolution MS or elemental analysis.

Green Chemistry

As everybody becomes more conscious of the effect we have on our environment, chemists have also been investigating a greener way of doing chemistry, and synthesis in particular. The problem can be approached in several ways:

- **Recycling:** A synthesis is devised in such a way that most solvents and reagents in a procedure can be recuperated at the end of the reaction, and therefore re-used for a subsequent reaction. For example, a reaction is run in toluene. Toluene is just the solvent. During the work-up of the reaction, the toluene can be recuperated, purified and used in another reaction.

- **Use water as solvent:** Chemists have been finding that many reactions can be run in water rather than in an organic solvent. An example is the Diels-Alder reaction, which in certain instances can be run even more efficiently in water than in an organic solvent. To maintain the green character of the reaction, the water should be purified at the end of the reaction.

- **Use no solvent:** In certain reactions, solvents can be avoided completely.

- **Atom economy:** The concept of atom economy was introduced by Prof. Barry Trost in the 1990s. The conversion efficiency of the starting material(s) to the product is calculated. How efficiently are all the atoms in the reagents used to form the product?

$$\% \text{ atom economy} = \frac{\text{MW product}}{\text{MW starting materials}} \times 100\ \%$$

An example of a highly efficient reaction would be a Diels-Alder reaction:

MW 82   MW 98   MW 180

$$\% \text{ atom economy} = \frac{180}{82 + 98} \times 100\ \% = 100\ \%$$

In this reaction, the two reagents are completely used in the product, and the % atom economy is therefore 100 %.

In a Fischer esterification, water is "lost" in the reaction:

MW 64   MW 88   MW 134

$$\% \text{ atom economy} = \frac{134}{64 + 88} \times 100 \% = 88 \%$$

At 88 %, this is still a highly economic reaction.

Here is the case of the Wittig reaction:

MW 360   MW 106   MW 104

Starting from the triphenylphosphonium bromide, which is treated with bu-tyl lithium, the resulting ylide is reacted with benzaldehyde, leading to the product styrene.

$$\% \text{ atom economy} = \frac{104}{360 + 106} \times 100 \% = 22 \%$$

So even though this is highly effective reaction, it is not an economic reaction.

- Use less hazardous chemicals if possible and practical.

- Design reaction for more efficient energy efficiency, i.e., design a reaction at room temperature or slightly above rather than 200 °C, for example.

- Use catalysts to make reactions more efficient.

- Minimize the use of large protecting groups.

Index

PERIODIC TABLE OF THE ELEMENTS

GROUP

Key:

11
Na
Sodium
22.99

- Atomic number
- Element symbol
- Element name
- Atomic mass

[x] = Mass number of the longest-lived isotope is given when the element does not have any stable nuclides.

State at standard temp and pressure (0 °C and 1 atm):

| Solid | Liquid | Gas | Unknown |

	1A	2A	3B	4B	5B	6B	7B		8B		1B	2B	3A	4A	5A	6A	7A	8A
	1	2	3	4	5	6	7	8	9	10	11	12	13	14	15	16	17	18
	IA	IIA	IIIB	IVB	VB	VIB	VIIB	VIIIB	VIIIB	VIIIB	IB	IIB	IIIA	IVA	VA	VIA	VIIA	VIIIA
1	1 H Hydrogen 1.008																	2 He Helium 4.00
2	3 Li Lithium 6.94	4 Be Beryllium 9.01											5 B Boron 10.81	6 C Carbon 12.01	7 N Nitrogen 14.01	8 O Oxygen 16.00	9 F Fluorine 19.00	10 Ne Neon 20.18
3	11 Na Sodium 22.99	12 Mg Magnesium 24.31											13 Al Aluminum 26.98	14 Si Silicon 28.09	15 P Phosphorus 30.97	16 S Sulfur 32.07	17 Cl Chlorine 35.45	18 Ar Argon 39.95
4	19 K Potassium 39.10	20 Ca Calcium 40.08	21 Sc Scandium 44.96	22 Ti Titanium 47.87	23 V Vanadium 50.94	24 Cr Chromium 52.00	25 Mn Manganese 54.94	26 Fe Iron 55.85	27 Co Cobalt 58.93	28 Ni Nickel 58.69	29 Cu Copper 63.55	30 Zn Zinc 65.38	31 Ga Gallium 69.72	32 Ge Germanium 72.64	33 As Arsenic 74.92	34 Se Selenium 78.96	35 Br Bromine 79.90	36 Kr Krypton 83.80
5	37 Rb Rubidium 85.47	38 Sr Strontium 87.62	39 Y Yttrium 88.91	40 Zr Zirconium 91.22	41 Nb Niobium 92.91	42 Mo Molybdenum 95.96	43 Tc Technetium [98]	44 Ru Ruthenium 101.07	45 Rh Rhodium 102.91	46 Pd Palladium 106.42	47 Ag Silver 107.87	48 Cd Cadmium 112.41	49 In Indium 114.82	50 Sn Tin 118.71	51 Sb Antimony 121.76	52 Te Tellurium 127.60	53 I Iodine 126.90	54 Xe Xenon 131.29
6	55 Cs Cesium 132.91	56 Ba Barium 137.33	57–71	72 Hf Hafnium 178.49	73 Ta Tantalum 180.95	74 W Tungsten 183.84	75 Re Rhenium 186.21	76 Os Osmium 190.23	77 Ir Iridium 192.22	78 Pt Platinum 195.08	79 Au Gold 196.97	80 Hg Mercury 200.59	81 Tl Thallium 204.38	82 Pb Lead 207.2	83 Bi Bismuth 208.98	84 Po Polonium [209]	85 At Astatine [210]	86 Rn Radon [222]
7	87 Fr Francium [223]	88 Ra Radium [226]	89–103	104 Rf Rutherfordium [261]	105 Db Dubnium [262]	106 Sg Seaborgium [266]	107 Bh Bohrium [264]	108 Hs Hassium [277]	109 Mt Meitnerium [268]	110 Ds Darmstadtium [271]	111 Rg Roentgenium [272]	112 Cn Copernicium [285]	113 Uut Ununtrium [284]	114 Uuq Ununquadium [289]	115 Uup Ununpentium [288]	116 Uuh Ununhexium [293]	117 Uus Ununseptium [294]	118 Uuo Ununoctium [294]

LANTHANIDES

57 La Lanthanum 138.91	58 Ce Cerium 140.12	59 Pr Praseodymium 140.91	60 Nd Neodymium 144.24	61 Pm Promethium [145]	62 Sm Samarium 150.36	63 Eu Europium 151.96	64 Gd Gadolinium 157.25	65 Tb Terbium 158.93	66 Dy Dysprosium 162.50	67 Ho Holmium 164.93	68 Er Erbium 167.26	69 Tm Thulium 168.93	70 Yb Ytterbium 173.05	71 Lu Lutetium 174.97

ACTINIDES

89 Ac Actinium [227]	90 Th Thorium 232.04	91 Pa Protactinium 231.04	92 U Uranium 238.03	93 Np Neptunium [237]	94 Pu Plutonium [244]	95 Am Americium [243]	96 Cm Curium [247]	97 Bk Berkelium [247]	98 Cf Californium [251]	99 Es Einsteinium [252]	100 Fm Fermium [257]	101 Md Mendelevium [258]	102 No Nobelium [259]	103 Lr Lawrencium [262]

ALKALI METALS
ALKALINE EARTH METALS
TRANSITION METALS
METALLOIDS
NON-METALS
NOBLE GASES
HALOGENS
RARE EARTH METALS
P-BLOCK METALS

PERIOD

Note: "Caesium" and "aluminium" are the internationally recognized spellings for "cesium" and "aluminum."

Source: *Pure and Applied Chemistry* **78** (11), 2051–2066 (2006); including August 2007 and February 2010 IUPAC updates.

HAYDEN McNEIL

09.01.10